P9-DMM-204

D0015306

SHE STAYS

HOW GOD INSPIRED A FRIENDSHIP THAT SAVED
BETTYE AND RICKY VAN SHELTON'S MARRIAGE

BETTYE SHELTON
AND
ANDY LANDIS
WITH CAROLE GIFT PAGE

A JANET THOMA BOOK

THOMAS NELSON PUBLISHERS
Nashville · Atlanta · London · Vancouver

Published in Nashville, Tennessee, by Thomas Nelson, Inc., Publishers, and distributed in Canada by Word Communications, Ltd., Richmond, British Columbia.

Library of Congress Cataloging-in-Publication Data

Shelton, Bettye, 1952–
    She stays / Bettye Shelton and Andy Landis.
        p.   cm.
    ISBN 0-7852-7742-0
    1. Shelton, Bettye.   2. Shelton, Ricky Van.   3. Country musicians—
United States—Biography.   4. Musicians' spouses—Religious life.
I. Landis, Andy.
ML420.—S5364A3   1995
782.42′1642′0922—dc20
    [B]   95-24555
                                                                            CIP

Printed in the United States of America.

1 2 3 4 5 6 — 00 99 98 97 96 95

I dedicate this book to my husband, Ricky Van Shelton. He is one of the finest people I have ever known, and I consider it an honor and a blessing to be his wife.

It is difficult for any of us to acknowledge our "darker" side, but to permit it to be documented for all to read requires an extremely unselfish and centered heart. Ricky's blessing on this project is a testimony to his desire to reach others with our message of hope and commitment. God bless you, husband.

B. S.

This work is dedicated to all of you who choose to help others even when it hurts; who choose to love even when it is not deserved; who choose to give even when it would be easier not to.

You know who you are.

May you be encouraged and honored by this book.

A.L.

ACKNOWLEDGMENTS FROM
BETTYE SHELTON

I am especially grateful to Carole Gift Page; her consideration and insight were extraordinary. I also wish to thank the staff at Janet Thoma Books for their encouragement and enthusiasm for this project . . . they have been such a joy to work with. Thanks, also, to Ken Stephens at Thomas Nelson Publishers for opening the door for Andy and me. And a special thanks to Lindsay and Richard for their prayers and friendship, to Gina for her support, and to Jerry and Linda for always being there for us.

My deepest gratitude goes to the hundreds of Ricky Van Shelton fans who have prayed for us over the years without knowing why; their dedication and love have sustained us more than they may ever know.

The appreciation I have for my co-author, Andy Landis, goes beyond my ability to express in words. I thank God daily for bringing her into my life. There have been times when I wondered if she may actually be my very own angel in the flesh who was sent to minister to me. I know now that she was sent to minister to thousands. I will treasure our personal friendship forever.

*C*arole Gift Page, your talent and human kindness are incredible. This book wouldn't be the same without you. Janet Thoma, thanks for being the champion of our project. Esther Fitzpatrick, you've been wonderful. Ken Stephens, thank you for believing. All of you at Thomas Nelson and Janet Thoma Books have made this experience easy for me.

Allen Brown, you have discovered by now that I am a late bloomer. Thanks for hanging in there. Jennie Carey, you helped more than you know. Thank you, David Thomas, for keeping my office in professional and spiritual order. I will miss you terribly.

God Bless you, Allen Shamblin, for writing the song "She Stays" with me. Thanks to Jonathon Watkins, Jill Landess, Velvet Rousseau and Brenda Boswell for encouraging me and my music through the storm.

Jerry Weimer . . . that plane ride! WOW . . . what a difference a seat makes! Jeff Teague, Rick Bowles and the staff at Word/Nashville and Epic Records . . . this is an honor for me.

To my family, my friends and my fans who believe in

me "no matter what." Please know that your love and prayers keep me going. The words "thank you" cannot express my gratitude.

Steve, you are a fine man . . . full of integrity and boldness. I don't know why God chose to bless me by making you my husband, but I am honored that He did.

A special thanks goes to my mom, Mildred Marion Rhodes Landis. You are the first person who taught me to love beyond measure. You taught me to be the kind of friend who could stay.

And finally to my co-author and friend, Bettye Shelton. You are an amazing woman. It was a privilege for me to have been called to your side . . . I wouldn't have missed it for the world.

*O*ut of the shadows he stepped into a circle of light, a solid, roughhewn man in black leather jacket and jeans, his trademark white Stetson slung low over his bronzed forehead, guitar in hand, cowboy boots clicking on a polished stage. Country boy and country music star Ricky Van Shelton—his handsome face chipped from granite—filled the stage with a dazzling, captivating energy. To a spellbound audience he crooned a hauntingly romantic ballad with his resonant baritone. His deep voice emerged full of sun and flint, the words flowing slow and golden and sweet as honey.

> *You've got me calling on the phone,*
> *You've got me crying all night long.*
> *But, baby, I love you. Baby, yes, I love you.*
> *Heard people saying lots of things*
> *'Bout how you sold your wedding ring,*
> *But, baby, I love you. Baby, yes, I love you.*
> *But I don't care what people say.*

I still love you anyway.
Oh, yes, I love you. I still love you. . . .

But the woman who waited at home for him on his 150-acre ranch outside of Nashville, Tennessee hadn't heard her husband speak of love for a very long time.

November 26, 1990

Bettye Shelton gripped the telephone receiver until her knuckles turned bone-white. She sat facing the wall, her back to the sprawling room filled with Ricky's treasures and mementos—primitive-style paintings, fifties model cars, Coca-Cola signs, cowboy memorabilia, even his life-size, cigar-store Indian. Inhaling sharply, she forced her mind to block out all the things surrounding her that spoke of Ricky—the cherished bits and pieces and odds and ends of Ricky's heart and soul. She dared not think of Ricky now.

She dialed the number again, then hung up before it rang. A clock ticked in the silence, or was it her own pounding heart, the sound of blood moving through her temples? She felt the pumping rhythm in her veins, steady, insistent, inevitable. Surge and retreat, surge and retreat, echoing the words pulsing in her head. *Do it! Don't! Do it! Don't!*

The early morning chill seeped through her skin, moving like mist through her mind, bringing gloom heavy and dark as fog. She had been faithful to Ricky always. Always. And it wasn't as if she intended to be unfaithful now.

Calling an old friend was a harmless gesture. It meant nothing. Reaching out to someone who had cared about her once, who surely still cared for her—what harm could it bring? She needed someone. Someone to remind her that she was pretty and appealing and worthwhile. Someone to notice the vivid blue of her eyes or the sheen of her auburn hair or the curve of her figure. She needed tenderness and romance to melt the cold rock of desperation that had been growing in her for months. If she was to survive, she needed to feel loved again!

But calling someone, inviting his attentions—did she dare go that far? This would be the first time in her eleven years with Ricky that she had reached out to another man —a man who would likely risk everything to be with her.

It was a bold, fanciful, unthinkable notion. But wouldn't it be worth it? He would make her feel everything missing in her relationship with Ricky—passion, intimacy, love, and desire. He would make her feel like a woman again. All she had to do was call. *Perhaps he'll come to Nashville to see me. We could see the sights and have dinner. A secluded spot with candlelight and roses. Or I could meet him in his hotel. No one would know. He would hold me and kiss me and tell me how much he wants me. But I wouldn't go to bed with him. I'd leave before . . . before . . . Oh, God, don't You understand? I need this! I need to feel desirable again!*

With trembling fingers Bettye dialed the number once more and listened as the line rang. All of her senses were alert to the point of pain. The ringing seemed shrill; it filled her head and her home, jarring—splintering—the silence, the sound as strident and oppressive as a death knell. She held her breath as she imagined him answering; she heard the sound of his voice in her head. And suddenly she knew with a sinking certainty that this romantic encounter would not stop with a few kisses and embraces. She was kidding herself. She would not be able to walk away. She would end up having an affair with this man!

A wave of nausea rose in her throat, sour as gall, twisting her stomach with revulsion and self-loathing. She slammed the receiver down and clasped her hand over her mouth. *Oh, my God, what am I doing? What's wrong with me? I'm about to abort my marriage! What have I become?*

She put her head in her hands and began to sob. She was going under, losing control, sinking, flailing, drowning. Aloud she begged, "Oh, my God, my God! Help me! Please help me! Help me!"

The telephone rang, startling her to silence. She stared at it in astonishment, then seized the receiver as if it were a lifeline. In a small, tentative voice, she whispered, "Hello?"

A bright, lyrical voice replied, "Hello, Bettye? This is Andy Landis. Remember me? I'm Steve Buckingham's fiancee."

Bettye's mind felt sluggish, dazed. After a long moment her memory clicked into place and she managed unevenly, "Oh, sure, Andy. How are you?"

"I'm just fine, Bettye. Um, are *you* okay?"

Bettye hadn't expected this sudden, gentle intrusion. She never answered her own phone; the answering machine screened all calls. Why this time had she picked up the receiver on its first ring?

"Bettye," Andy continued softly, "I thought you might need someone to talk to. I just have this feeling that you're feeling bad, and I . . . well, I'd just like to be there for you."

How did she know? Bettye's tears started again, flowing, surging, breaking the dam of her emotions. "Oh, Andy," she cried, "I'm so glad you called. You don't know what I was about to do. You just don't know what I was about to do!"

For two weeks Andy Landis hadn't been able to get Bettye Shelton off her mind. Considering she hardly knew Bettye, her preoccupation was strange. They had met only twice before. The first time was last summer on Ricky's bus after a performance. Andy's fiancé, Steve Buckingham, a producer with Columbia Records, had discovered Ricky Van Shelton four years before and had played a pivotal role in making him a country music star. Since then, Steve and Ricky had continued to work together professionally, but more than that, they had become close friends.

Although Andy hardly recalled that first meeting with Bettye, their second encounter on November 9th haunted her even now, two weeks later. She remembered that evening as if it were yesterday. With Ricky away on tour, Bettye's friends, Jerry and Linda Thompson, had invited Steve and Andy to join them in celebrating Bettye's birthday at the Cherokee Steak House in Gallatin, Tennessee. The conversation around the table had been light and jovial. Jerry told the funniest stories, one after another, and everyone laughed and laughed.

But Andy couldn't help noticing Bettye's expression. Yes, she laughed with the rest of them, but when she stopped laughing, a sadness settled over her face, and her striking blue eyes revealed oceans of pain.

Doesn't anybody notice this? Andy had wondered. *She can't even look me in the eye. Am I the only one who sees how much she's hurting?*

Driving home from the party that night, Andy told Steve, "Something's wrong with Bettye."

"Wrong?" He sounded skeptical. "What could be wrong?"

"I don't know. I just know she's not happy."

"Don't you think you're just being overly sensitive?"

"Yes, I'm overly sensitive," Andy returned. "That's how I know something's wrong."

"She's probably just missing Ricky. You know how it is. He's out on tour for weeks at a time."

"No, it's more than that. Something's wrong. I feel it."

"You're making too much of this, honey. Try and forget it."

But she hadn't forgotten. In fact, as the days passed, Andy's burden for Bettye had grown heavier. She found herself waking in the middle of the night thinking of Bettye, praying for her. Sometimes she woke up weeping for this woman she hardly knew. Now, two weeks after the party, Bettye was on her mind all the time. Bettye's pain had become Andy's pain.

Andy knew what she had to do. Telephone Bettye. But when she approached Steve with the idea on Sunday evening, November 25th, he was less than enthusiastic.

"Do you think that's wise? You know how the business is. Celebrities value their privacy above all else."

She had gazed for a long moment at her fiancé before remarking, "It's all so superficial, isn't it, Steve? You can't just look people in the eye and say, 'How are you? I mean, how are you *really*?' You've got to say, 'What are you doing now?' Meaning, 'Are you working on a record? . . . Are you writing a book? . . . Are you making a movie?' Why must it all be so terribly impersonal?"

Steve raked his fingers through his thick brown hair and shrugged. He was a tall, imposing man, broad-shouldered and solidly built, yet lean and trim. He was a handsome man, but Andy had fallen in love with his uncompromising honesty and integrity. He spoke now with a quiet, polished confidence. "Like I said, Andy, celebrities guard their privacy. It's the one thing they no longer have."

"I know, I know. Public figures must have their boundaries. Their best friend could be the next person to call *The National Enquirer*." She drew in a sharp breath and said solemnly, "But I can't get Bettye off my mind, Steve. I'm worried about her. Do you think she has somebody to talk to? Does anyone check on her to make sure she's okay?"

"I'm sure someone does. She has friends. She has Ricky. And they both have big families with strong ties."

"What about Ricky? Is he okay?"

S H E   S T A Y S

Steve's brow furrowed. "I'm not sure. Lately he's been moody, distant. Drinking too much."

Andy nodded. "I've heard the rumors on Music Row."

"Being on the road isn't easy. His career's in high gear. A lot's at stake. The pressure's on."

"What about the pressures on Bettye? I know she's hurting, Steve. I saw it in her face. I've got to call her and see if I can help."

Steve reached for her hand and pulled her over beside him. "You've got so much love and concern for other people, Andy. I love that about you. But be careful. Ricky and I work together. I don't want this to get awkward."

"Are you saying I shouldn't call her?"

He looked her squarely in the eyes. "No. I'm just saying I love you and I trust you, but you'd better know what you're doing."

Andy felt an icy grip around her stomach. She grew silent in his arms. Steve was right. She didn't want Ricky to think she was meddling in his affairs. It could strain, even jeopardize, his relationship with Steve. Nothing was worth putting her fiancé's career at risk. Steve would have every right to get angry with her, perhaps even break up with her.

She had waited all of her life for a man like Steve Buckingham. And they had already weathered so much together—a long-distance romance and broken engagement, plus the shattering diagnosis last spring of the malignant melanoma in her leg, followed by surgery and an exhausting recuperation.

Now, at long last, the trials and heartaches were behind her. Andy's life was back on track. Steve was right, she had to be careful. Too often she had played Joan of Arc, running with her emotions, throwing caution to the wind, rushing in to help where others feared to tread. No more. It was time to put Andy Landis first.

Silently she vowed not to let anything interfere with the happiness she'd found—not even the sad, soulful eyes of a lovely, lonely lady named Bettye Shelton.

But Andy's resolve was short-lived; her burden for Bettye could not be argued or reasoned away. It remained —a pressing, relentless irritant to her soul, like a pebble in a shoe or a grain of sand in the eye.

That night Andy got down on her knees and declared, "God, if this is from You, if You want me to put myself into Bettye's life, then make it clear to me when I wake up in the morning. If this is not from You, then take this feeling away. I don't know anymore what's me and what's You. So if You want me to call her, You've got to make it absolutely clear."

The next morning when Andy opened her eyes, her first thought was, *Bettye is in so much pain. Okay, I'll call her. Whatever You say, Lord. I'll call her today.*

Immediately, peace spread through her like sunshine.

When she telephoned Steve for Bettye's number, he gave it with a brief admonition. "Please, Andy, be tactful. Keep the business out of it."

She promised she would.

For the next hour Andy paced the kitchen with phone in hand, her mouth dry and heart thumping as she argued with herself. *What am I doing? I'm overstepping my bounds. This woman will say "Andy who?" Or "Who do you think you are, suggesting I don't have my life together?" Or* worse, she might tell Ricky, *"Your producer's fiancee is bothering me. Tell Steve to call off his wacky girlfriend!"*

Stop it, Andy. Forget about yourself. Someone's drowning, screaming for help. Her silence is one of the most painful screams you've ever heard. You can't stand by and not do something to save her!

Andy gulped, took a deep breath, and started to dial. She hung up. *Not yet. What am I going to say?*

Suddenly she felt as if God Himself were tapping her on the shoulder and commanding, *NOW!* She dialed the number and Bettye answered on the first ring.

Andy heard the pain in Bettye's voice when she answered, as stark and poignant as the pain had been in her eyes. That's why she'd asked, "Are *you* okay?"

When there was no response Andy plunged on. "I thought you might need someone to talk to. I just have this feeling that you're feeling bad, and I . . . well, I'd just like to be there for you."

Bettye began to weep. Between sobs, she said, "Oh, Andy, I'm so glad you called. You don't know what I was about to do. You just don't know what I was about to do!"

Andy's heart leapt in alarm. *Oh, no, she's going to kill herself!* "Listen, Bettye, can I come to see you? Or would you like to come here?"

Bettye's voice sounded stronger. "Why don't you come to my house this weekend, Andy, and spend the night."

Andy felt a surge of joy and relief. *Thank You, God! You did it!* Quelling her excitement, she declared, "Give me directions, and I'll be there!"

After hanging up the phone, Andy danced and

20

SHELTON & LANDIS

shouted like a child at Christmas. "Thank You, God! She's open to this! I'll have a chance to help her! Thank You!"

But she might not have danced with such gleeful abandon had she known how long and hard the journey would be, where it would take her, and the price she would pay.

CHAPTER 2

Bettye woke early on Saturday morning, her mind already burdened with anxiety. Her houseguest, Andy Landis, would be arriving that evening. For the life of her, she didn't know why she had invited this stranger to come here to the farm and actually spend the night. Who was this girl anyway? Buck's girlfriend, yes. For that reason alone Bettye would have to be a gracious hostess. After all, Steve Buckingham was Ricky's friend and producer at Columbia Records. But what did anyone really know about his fiancee, except that she was from Los Angeles? Los Angeles! That could mean anything!

Bettye stood at her kitchen counter and fixed herself a bowl of cereal. The house was quiet. It was always quiet. And so often lonely. She gazed out the window at the rolling hills and thickets of white birch washed with the first pale rays of morning light. The December frost had turned the chilled earth a muted gray-green. A thin patina of ice glistened on the raw, coarse timber of the wrap-around porch.

No other houses were visible for a mile, except for the little cabin Ricky had tenderly moved log by log and stone by stone from a neighboring farm to his own property. They had no close neighbors—just the Cumberland River meandering lazily beside their immense log farmhouse and the herd of beefalo grazing in the nearby pastures.

This house was the refuge Ricky had always longed for. He loved this land, this lush, pristine wilderness, with its acres of forests and rivers, placid lakes and granite cliffs, and sweeping, wide open grasslands as far as the eye could see. Ironic and sad that he had so little time to spend here.

Bettye took her cereal bowl over to the breakfast nook and sat down where she could gaze out at the river and, beside it, their screened, natural-wood gazebo with its cedar-shake roof. Ricky's family and hers had come together and built the gazebo for them the summer before last. It was a special memory, a time when she and Ricky were still close.

Bettye could tell already that this was going to be a nice day, clear and crisp and just biting enough to bring the senses alive. A cozy, wintry day—the kind of day to sit and read by a toasty fire or to bundle up and take a walk in the woods and let the sharp, clean air put roses in your cheeks.

But she was having company. Someone she didn't even know. What would they talk about? What would they do?

No doubt Andy would expect Bettye to pour out her heart and tell her all her troubles. But that had never been Bettye's style. It was hard enough sharing her problems with close friends and family she'd known and loved forever.

In fact, she hadn't quite admitted to herself that there

were problems. No one's life was perfect. Marriages weren't perfect. Even when you got everything you thought you ever wanted, you realized it was really a trade-off. Every time you gained something, you gave up something just as precious. Ricky had discovered that. The more fame and success he achieved, the more of himself he had to give up. Bettye was learning that bitter lesson too. Every day she seemed to lose more of Ricky. And lately it looked as if nothing could bring him back.

That's why it was easier to close her eyes or look the other way and pretend she wasn't hurting. For so long now she had guarded her pain, taking care not to probe the wound too deeply, lest the hurt flow unchecked, beyond anyone's power to heal.

And now—now this strange woman would breeze in, ready to do her good deed and thinking she had all the answers. Bettye was cornered, trapped by her own hand. Fear moved in her with a glacial chill as she imagined the two of them facing an awkward weekend of solitude.

How had she gotten herself into this dilemma? A shard of memory brought back the hurtful phone call she had almost made. Shame warmed her face even now. Andy had kept her from making a terrible mistake, and in that emotionally charged moment Bettye had let down her guard and admitted she needed help.

And for that momentary lapse she must now face this idealistic young woman who wanted to rush in and save her.

Bettye Shelton didn't need saving.

She was feeling better now. Stronger, calmer, less shaken by the changing winds of her own emotions. She

24

didn't need Andy's help. She could manage her own life quite well, thank you.

But it was too late to withdraw the invitation. It would be rude and inhospitable. And Andy might conclude that she had something to hide. No, she couldn't cancel. But perhaps there was another solution.

The idea came to her in an instant. She would throw a party. She would telephone a few of her friends and invite them over for the evening. Then she would telephone Andy and kindly explain that company was coming, so perhaps she might want to schedule her visit for another time. Truth be told, maybe Andy herself was having reservations and looking for a way out.

For the first time that morning Bettye's anxiety gave way to anticipation. She would make this evening a real celebration. Christmas was only weeks away. Why not get a tree and decorate it! "I want to have a Christmas," she said aloud, to no one. "Ricky and I haven't had a real tree since moving to Nashville. We're always in Virginia for the holidays. Six years it's been! But this year we're gonna have us a real tree!"

Her spirits lifting, she went to the phone and telephoned her friends, Carolyn and Rick Kitts, and invited them and their three small children over. "Tonight I want this big, empty house to ring with the laughter of children," she said expansively. Then she called Jerry and Aleta Daugherty. "I know your baby's due next month, Aleta, but I sure hope you can come on over and help me decorate a Christmas tree."

When Bettye had safely lined up her guests, she telephoned Andy and said in her most apologetic tone, "I sure hope you don't mind, Andy. I'm having a few close friends over for a little Christmas party tonight. I figured you might feel more comfortable getting together another time . . ." She let her voice trail off. What she was really saying was, *See, Andy? I'm a happy woman. I've got my friends, I'm decorating for Christmas. My life is full. Why would you think I need to talk to you about anything?*

With a jolt Bettye realized Andy's response wasn't what she had expected. "Why, that sounds just wonderful, Bettye," Andy said in her soft, lyrical voice. "Sure, I'd just love to come and meet your friends. That'll be so much fun! I'll see you about seven."

"Seven will be fine," Bettye mumbled, thinking, *Oh, shoot!* But another small part of her seized on a shred of hope: *She didn't back down! She really wants to help. And she's the only one who's noticed how much I'm hurting!*

That afternoon Bettye drove to a garden center in Lebanon and bought the most beautiful blue spruce she could find—a perfectly formed eight footer with long needles and full, lush branches. "It's exactly right!" she declared as two attendants lifted the huge tree into the back of her pickup.

She drove to Wal-Mart, then to a little craft shop and purchased strings of plain white lights, red garlands, Victorian angels, and old-fashioned, shiny red bulbs. She would make this a lovely Victorian Christmas. And for the top of the tree she bought a large clear star with a white light, because Ricky loved five-pointed stars. Funny. Even when he wasn't there, she was still thinking of Ricky.

———◆———

Andy was running late. When she had borrowed Steve's car to drive out to Bettye's, she hadn't realized how long the drive would be. It was almost dark now, and the houses were getting sparser and the foliage thicker with every mile.

She knew from their earlier conversation that Bettye really didn't want her to come, but then Bettye didn't know Andy Landis, the eternal optimist. If Andy had stopped every time she heard the word *no*, she wouldn't have accomplished half the things she'd done in her life. When she auditioned for a part and heard, "No, you're the wrong type, the wrong color, the wrong size," whatever, she just told herself, *You're going to hear a lot of nos until you get to yes, sooner or later!*

She started singing in her rich, smooth alto, then let the melody drift off as she prayed for God's blessing on the evening ahead. She wanted to be ready, available, prepared to say just the right words. She would trust God's Spirit to undergird her all the way.

And then, through the thickets and trees she saw it in the distance—the Shelton farmhouse—a huge, imposing silhouette in the shadows; a massive fortress made of roughhewn logs set on a rolling hill beside a winding river. She followed the gravel driveway a half mile until she came to a sprawling front yard. To the left stood a long red barn and to the right a quaint little log cabin beside a small tilled garden. Even in the darkening twilight, it was one of the most rustic, picturesque scenes Andy had ever glimpsed.

By the time Andy stepped inside the farmhouse, the party was well underway and the guests, comfortably dressed in sweatshirts and jeans, were already decorating a huge Christmas tree. Andy could smell the rich aromas of coffee and spicy chili mixing with the fresh scent of pine needles and the toasty smell of logs burning in the massive stone fireplace at the far end of the room. The spacious room, with its high-beamed cathedral ceiling of knotty pine, stretched from kitchen to dining room to living room. Fine-grained natural wood was everywhere —in the burnished-gold paneling, the polished hardwood floors, the gleaming, finely crafted cabinets.

As Bettye led the way over to her guests, Andy gazed around, captivated. The decor was casual, homey, and fascinatingly eclectic—overstuffed sofa and recliner rockers accented by a pastiche of antique tables and lamps, cowboy trappings, and forties, fifties, and sixties memorabilia. The only hint that this was the home of a country music star was seen in the long hallway displaying dozens of framed gold and platinum records and other awards. Above the doorway was a street sign that read RICKY VAN SHELTON BLVD.

In her softly genteel voice, Bettye made the introductions. "Everyone, this is Andy Landis. She's engaged to Buck, Ricky's producer at Columbia Records. Andy, this is Rick and Carolyn Kitts. Carolyn's the one who actually brought me to Nashville in '84. She hired me to head up the personnel department at her company, Alcon Surgical Division."

Andy offered her hand to the tall, exotic brunette, then to the strapping, blond lumberjack of a man beside her.

"Those three beautiful children sitting under the Christmas tree belong to them," said Bettye with a smile.

Carolyn laughed. "They're already waiting for Santa!"

"And this is Jerry and Aleta Daugherty." Bettye nodded toward an attractive blond couple in their twenties. "Aleta worked with Carolyn and me. She and Jerry still act like newlyweds, and they're expecting their first child almost any day now."

Aleta patted her rounded tummy and smiled. "Hopefully it won't be tonight."

Andy smiled back and extended her hand. She already felt at home with these friendly, down-to-earth people. She could tell that the mood tonight was going to be warm and convivial.

After a moment Aleta asked, "Are you from Nashville, Andy?"

"Los Angeles. But I live and work in Nashville now. I'm a staff writer with Warner/Chappell. I write songs—and sing."

"You look familiar. Have you been on TV?"

Andy nodded. "I've done commercials and some television parts."

"I knew I'd seen you!"

Bettye clasped Andy's arm. "Bless your heart, Andy, I didn't know you were an actress and a singer. Buck's been holding out on us!"

"You and Aleta can lead us singing Christmas carols," said Jerry, picking up one of Ricky's guitars. "We can use all the pretty voices we can get. Rick and I like to sing loud."

They spent the next several hours gathered around the Christmas tree singing carols and gospel songs, swapping stories, drinking eggnog, and laughing until their sides ached. Andy stole occasional glances at Bettye and noted that she looked beautiful—her deep auburn hair tousled and framing her face just so, her expression animated, her complexion rosy and glowing from the warmth of the fire. Andy noticed that Bettye was watching her, too, and she had a feeling she'd passed all of Bettye's tests. She'd won over her friends; she felt as comfortable as if they'd been socializing together all their lives. Even the Kitts's children—a boy and two girls—had clambered up on Andy's lap.

When everyone was "sung out," Bettye said, "If anybody's still hungry, you all go help yourselves to that pot of chili on the stove. If you're tired of chili, there's a bowl heaping with popcorn and plenty more eggnog."

Andy stood up and stretched. "Who wants something? I'll do the honors."

Bettye gazed curiously at her. "Andy, I just remembered. Weren't you walking with a cane when I met you last summer?"

She nodded. "I'd just had surgery on my leg."

"That's right. Buck said you had quite a time of it."

"I had a malignant melanoma. It was scary, but I'm fine now." She laughed lightly. "In fact, people call me the melanoma expert because I'm always looking at everyone's moles. Now who wants more eggnog? Or are we all ready for another verse of 'Silent Night' or 'Tennessee Waltz'?"

Again, a chorus of cheery, convivial laughter.

It was nearly midnight when Bettye's guests finally said their good-byes and headed out the door—the Daughertys first, followed by the Kitts carrying their slumbering children in their arms. Both Andy and Bettye stood on the sprawling front porch waving farewell and wishing the two families safety on the road. So at ease had they all grown with one another that they could have

30

been Andy's houseguests as easily as Bettye's. Andy sensed she had truly gained a handful of new friends tonight.

But now it was time for her real mission to begin. She turned and looked at Bettye.

Bettye looked back expectantly and let out a sigh, a glimmer of emotion glinting in her blue eyes. "Well . . . ?"

"Bettye," Andy said softly, "let's talk."

CHAPTER 3

*T*he house was so silent it seemed that time stood still, hushed and poised, waiting for this midnight hour. The world had receded into wintry, slumbering shadows. Nothing existed except two women who knew the time had come to talk from the heart.

They sat in the living room by the fireplace, sipping mugs of strong, hot tea—Bettye curled on the sofa, Andy relaxing in the rocking chair. The room was dark except for the fire's glowing embers and the gleaming white lights from the tree. The zesty aroma of crackling logs mingled with the pungent scent of pine needles, creating an ambiance of peace and safety and good will.

Bettye looked over and smiled at Andy. She had dreaded this moment, and yet now she felt surprisingly comfortable with this lithe blonde woman who effused such spontaneity and warmth. It was as if they had known each other for years. In a few brief hours Andy had passed all of Bettye's silly little tests and had won her trust. "You were a real hit tonight, Andy," she said in her melodic Southern cadence. "My friends loved you."

Andy returned the smile. "I loved them too. They're wonderful people. It was a terrific party."

"Well, you made it special—and fun."

"Oh, Bettye, you made it special—and this house! It's incredible. So peaceful and beautiful." Andy gazed around at the darkened room etched with a soft, rosy fireglow. "The tranquillity here is awesome."

Bettye's voice took on a somber tone, faintly remote, as if she were thinking aloud. "This house isn't beautiful to me."

Andy sounded surprised. "How can you say that? Of course it's—"

"I wish we had never built this house."

"Bettye, what are you saying?"

"I hate this house. Ricky and I were happy before we moved here. This house has driven us apart."

The silence had changed. It was uneasy now; an undercurrent of tension charged the air. The silence was too loud for Bettye to bear. She could tell by Andy's expression that she was shocked. *What must she think of me now? That I'm ungrateful, complaining, crazy? Why didn't I just play along instead of uttering the truth—that I loathe this house Ricky built me!*

Andy slowly sipped her tea, then set the ceramic mug on the table beside her. "Why do you feel that way?"

Tears welled up in Bettye's eyes. "Oh, Andy, this was going to be our dream house. Instead, it's turned out to be a nightmare! When Ricky and I started out together, we had a little trailer in Grit, Virginia, where Ricky was born and raised. His folks still live there. We lived in this little itty-bitty place, but we were so in love and so happy together.

"But when we built this house, there was so much stress. It took more time and energy and money than we planned, putting more pressure on Ricky. We moved in last Valentine's Day. Ricky was on the road, so I had to move us in. Now he's gone all the time earning the money to pay for this place, and I'm here alone in this huge house, feeling lonely and miserable."

Bettye lapsed into a troubled silence and realized she was shivering. She got up, stoked the dying embers and put another log on the fire, then sat back down and sipped her tea.

"I know it sounds awful, Andy," she continued dolefully, "but every day I look at this house and think, *I traded my peace of mind for you!* I hate living here. I wish we had the trailer back. I wish we still lived in our little two-bedroom house in Nashville. I'd give up this house in a heartbeat if we could have the love we had before."

"Oh, Bettye!" Andy met her gaze with a directness that unnerved her. "Bettye, you're so wrong about this house!"

Bettye was dumbfounded. Had she heard right? She had expected at least a small measure of sympathy and commiseration. Instead, Andy had rebuked her. "Wrong? How?" she managed.

Andy gazed around and opened her hands expansively. "Bettye, there's so much life here, so much of God's creation! This is a shelter for you and Ricky from the world outside. Look at all this awesome wood. Look at the fine grains and the rich colors. And the warmth! Your house is so warm and inviting. Look at those big smooth stones in your fireplace—what a lovely blue-gray they are. All of this has come together just for you and Ricky."

Bettye listened, her eyes riveted on Andy.

"There's so much peace in these walls," Andy went on, her voice gentle but firm with conviction. "You've got to feel how much this house loves you and is taking care of you. You've got to feel that."

Bettye followed Andy's gaze around the room. Strangely, she felt as if she were seeing her house for the first time—through Andy's eyes! All along she had been looking at her house with bitterness and resentment, but now Andy was showing its beauty to her. For the first time she felt cradled, warmed, and embraced by these walls. She admired the gleaming panels, the sturdy beams, the little knotholes, and the rich, smooth grains. Suddenly it all came alive to her.

Tears spilled out of Bettye's eyes and ran freely down her cheeks. Her heart swelled with rivers of gratitude. She was too filled with emotion to speak, but inside she was shouting, *Oh, Andy, you've given me the most precious gift —a love for my home!*

Andy's eyes remained fixed on Bettye. "The hurt you're feeling, it really has nothing to do with this house, does it?"

Bettye sipped her tea. It was lukewarm now. She turned the ceramic mug in her hands. It still felt pleasantly warm against her palms. Her voice was tenuous. "No, it's not the house. You've helped me see that. I guess I've known it all along. The real problem is Ricky and me. I know it's the pressure of his career, but the truth is, he's been cold and distant since we moved here. Lately he's stopped talking to me. He's stopped touching me. He won't even look me in the eyes. Sometimes I wake up in the middle of the night in tears because he won't touch me. He hears me crying and just turns his back to me. I love my husband, but I'm losing him, Andy. I'm losing him."

There was a heavy moment of silence before Bettye said with conviction, "It wasn't always like this, Andy. Ricky and I used to be so good together. We grew up in the same neck of the woods—him in Grit, Virginia, me in Altavista, just three or four miles apart. As teenagers we even visited each other's church sometimes. He was a little doll, and oh, could he sing! We were best friends for years before we fell in love. We had so much fun together, always laughing and talking and riding down old country dirt roads for hours at a time. We'd go swimming in the rock quarry, and he was such a gentleman, he'd even turn his head when I wore my string bikini. He'd put his shirt on when we went in a country store, and he'd turn his radio down when we drove by a church. And he'd never turn around in somebody's driveway, because he thought it was an intrusion of their privacy."

Bettye's voice grew wistful and reminiscent, as if she had almost forgotten Andy was there. "From the time I was a young girl I thought Ricky Shelton was wonderful. So kind and thoughtful. And sort of shy and bashful and reserved. When we were just friends—before we fell in love—he'd never come on to me. He was a real humble, simple man. And modest. I remember the first time he got out his guitar and sang me some of the songs he wrote. I'd heard him sing in church and knew he was good, but when he sang to me, I was just captivated. I

36

told him, 'Ricky, you've got to do something about this. People who make records have to hear you.'"

"And he said, 'Well, I've been to Nashville several times with friends of mine, but nothing ever came of it.'"

"And I said, 'Ricky, your music's gotta be heard. You were meant to be a singer, and not just in a country band singing on weekends.' And I guess that's when his dream became my dream."

Bettye's voice was tender with nostalgia. "By '79 Ricky and I knew we were meant to be together. On Labor Day we moved into a big old farmhouse in Stone Mountain, Virginia, and lived there for five years. I had a good job as a personnel assistant with Abbott Laboratories and went to school part-time. Ricky worked as a pipe fitter and sang on weekends at little country nightclubs and Ramada Inns and Moose Lodges, things like that. And the whole time we kept saying we had to get to Nashville.

"In December of '84, we finally moved to Nashville and rented us a little house close to Opryland. I went to work for Carolyn Kitts at Alcon, the lady you met tonight, Andy. I worked sometimes twelve hours a day while Ricky stayed home cleaning house and cooking suppers and working on his music in his little basement studio. Sometimes I came home so late, Ricky would tuck me into bed and then take off and go to local nightclubs, carrying homemade tapes of his songs. Some of the clubs let him get up and sing on amateur night, and he'd get home about three in the morning—just a few hours before I had to get up and start my day all over again.

"In those days Ricky made lots of contacts, but he didn't have any luck until Linda Thompson, my assistant at work, took one of his tapes home to her husband, Jerry."

"Of course!" said Andy. "Jerry and Linda Thompson —the couple who invited Steve and me to your birthday dinner."

"That's right," said Bettye. "Jerry's a columnist for *The Tennessean.* He knows everybody in Nashville and everybody knows Jerry. But at first he didn't want to listen to Ricky's tape. He told Linda, 'I've lived here all my life and never got mixed up in the music industry, and I don't intend to start now. Everybody and their brother would be after me if I started helping out wannabe country music singers.'

"But Linda fooled him. One day she just started playing Ricky's songs, and he said, 'Who's that?' And she said, 'It's the fella I've been trying to get you to listen to. Can we invite him over for a barbecue?' And he said okay. So Ricky and I went to their house for a cookout and Ricky took his guitar. He and Jerry hit it off like they'd known each other all their lives. Like two peas in a pod. And Ricky sang every country song I reckon he ever knew that night. Jerry didn't want him to stop. He said, 'I'm gonna help this boy!'

"So he started taking Ricky around Nashville to all the people in the music industry, and he got Columbia Records to agree to a showcase to hear Ricky perform. And—you probably know this already, Andy—afterwards, Jerry introduced Ricky to your fiancé, Buck, who was Artist and Repertoire vice-president at the time, and to Rick Blackburn, vice-president. Rick told Ricky, 'We're interested. We want to put you in the studio and see how you do.' They were just going to have him do a single, but once he got in the studio they were so blown away they went ahead and did a whole album. That was 'Wild-Eyed Dream.'

"In June of '86 he signed his contract with Columbia Records, and suddenly he was on his way. Hired himself a manager. Hired a lawyer. Hired accountants. And I thought, *Ricky's career's about to break; it's about to happen for him. And I want to be more than just Ricky's girl-friend. We've been together seven years. I don't feel like a girlfriend. I feel married. Like a wife!*

"Up until that time we figured we were happier than most married couples we knew. We kept saying, 'Well, if we don't get married, we won't get divorced.' But now Ricky was signing up all these people, and I wanted to be signed up too. And Ricky's daddy was calling and saying, 'Boy, why don't you marry that girl?' Fact is, his folks were never happy about us living in sin. Neither were mine.

"Ricky still didn't figure we needed a piece of paper, but I did. So he said, 'Okay, but I don't want no big deal. I want it real quiet. Let's just go somewhere and get married and let's not tell anybody.' And I said, 'All right, that's fine.'

"And I remember going to work that day—it was August 4th—and telling them I needed the afternoon off. I said, 'Ricky and I are going to the courthouse to get married.' Well, Linda Thompson called her husband, and Jerry called Ricky and said, 'If you want me to, I'm an ordained minister. I can marry you.' So we went to Springfield, where Jerry and Linda lived, and got married at the Wedding Chapel. I wore a short pink dress, and Linda and Carolyn bought me a beautiful bouquet. Ricky

39

wore a flowered pink Hawaiian shirt, blue jeans, cowboy boots, and a cowboy hat. It ended up being a nice little wedding, and I went back to work the next day.

"And, of course, Ricky worked constantly on his songs, and his voice got so strong and powerful. I remember the first time he went into the studio to work, Buck said to him, 'From this day on, Ricky, I want you to think like a star, walk like a star, dress like a star, do everything as if you were a star already.'"

Andy laughed lightly. "That sounds just like Steve."

"Well, what he said made a big impact on Ricky. It really did. You tell Buck—" Bettye smiled. "I know he's *Steve* to you, but he's *Buck* to us. You tell Buck, Ricky never forgot."

Andy rocked back and forth in her chair with a steady, languid motion. "I guess after Ricky's album came out, life must have changed drastically for you."

"It did. In 1985 Ricky's income was just seventy dollars. Can you believe it? In 1986, everything broke loose. The buzz word all over Nashville was Ricky Van Shelton, the new artist, the new singer. It was so exciting. Our dreams were finally coming true, Andy. Every time we turned around Ricky was winning another award. Every single was becoming a number one hit, every album was selling over a million units. Last year alone Ricky won thirteen awards from the music industry."

She paused, and her tone darkened. "But when you have a dream, you only think about the good side, not the bad side. You don't get something without having to give up something. I remember last year at the Nashville Network Music City News Awards Show. Ricky won four awards. We were really thrilled about the first two. Ricky jumped out of his seat and ran up on stage and got each award. But by the third one, he had this scared look on his face, and by the fourth one, I started crying. He whispered, 'It's too much.' I knew what he meant. We were both thinking, *Oh, no, how much are we going to have to give up now? There's not going to be anything left of us!*

"On the way home he said, 'Bettye, you know what's gonna happen? I thought we'd given up everything we had to give up, but they're gonna want more from us.' And he was right.

"Every year the pressure gets to him a little more. It's hard being away from home, touring all the time, and having so many people making demands on him. He's the kind of person who needs his home to keep him centered. He's a solitary man. The problem is, now he's built this wall around himself nobody can break through. Not even me."

Bettye ran her fingertip around the rim of her mug. She didn't even know why she was telling Andy all of this. It was as if, once the dam was opened, she had to let it all out—the pain and despair that had been building in her for months. "I don't think Ricky means to shut me out. He described it to me once that when he was out in public, on the road, everybody wanted him, everybody was reaching and touching and trying to get a piece of him. And he said every time somebody touched him, every time somebody shook his hand, every time somebody got in his face, he could feel a little piece of him leaving. It was like they were taking and taking and taking. So he started building up this wall so people couldn't keep taking from him.

"So now, when Ricky comes home, he doesn't see

me, he doesn't hear me, he doesn't even touch me. And when I ask what's wrong, he just says, 'Leave me alone. I need some time. I need a little bit of time.' That's what I meant earlier, Andy, when I said I think I'm losing him."

Bettye turned her gaze to the fireplace. The flames had died again to a flickering orange glow in the charred logs. The house was cold and the shadows in the room had deepened. But she still hadn't said all she needed to say. "When you telephoned me, Andy, and asked if I needed someone to talk to, I was feeling so desperate, I . . ." She paused, aware of the tremor in her voice. She willed herself not to cry. "I was so desperate, I was about to call a man I once knew. I was about to . . . have an affair."

Andy stopped rocking and let out a little sigh of relief.

Bettye looked at her as if to say, *You're not shocked by my confession?*

Andy rolled her eyes. "Oh, Bettye, I thought you were going to kill yourself!"

They exchanged a wry, abashed smile. After a few moments Bettye said, "I wasn't that desperate, Andy. But I am troubled. I don't know how to help Ricky. And with Ricky's career in . . ."

"Wait a minute, Bettye." Andy sat forward and looked deep into Bettye's eyes. Gently she said, "Listen, Bettye, I think there's something you need to understand. I didn't come here to talk about Ricky and his career. We've talked about him long enough. I came here to talk about *you*. I want to hear what you're doing to keep yourself busy. I want to know how *you* feel about things. Your plans for the future. Tell me what's important to *you*."

Bettye stared back blankly for a moment, startled. She

42

wasn't prepared for this. *Everybody* wanted to know about Ricky. She was always answering questions about him. Even her own family wanted to know, "What's Ricky doing now? How long has he been gone? Where's he touring? When's he coming back? How long did he stay home last time?"

A smile spread slowly across Bettye's lips and she felt moisture glisten in her eyes. "You want to know about me? Bless your heart, Andy. There's not a lot to tell. Two years ago I gave up my job to stay home and take care of Ricky. And that's what I've been doing ever since."

"What job was that?"

"I was a corporate personnel manager for two plants in Gallatin. But Ricky and I didn't need the money anymore, so I retired. I still hadn't received my degree though, so I signed up for classes at Belmont University in Nashville."

"Really? What are you studying?"

"Music business."

Andy cocked her head just so, her expression pensive, as if she were weighing Bettye's words. "Do you find that interesting?"

Bettye hesitated. "Well, yes. Of course. It's our whole livelihood, so I figured I should know something about it."

"What do you want to do when you finish?"

Bettye sat back. "I . . . I'm not sure what I'm going to do with it. I don't really have a plan. I guess I'll just continue to take care of the house and be a wife to Ricky."

Suddenly Andy sat up straight, her muscles flexed, ready for action, as if by the carriage of her own body she were trying to arrive at some hidden truth. "If you could do anything you wanted to do, Bettye, what would you do?"

Without thinking, Bettye said, "I want children."

"Well, great! Wonderful!" Andy waved her hands like a genie granting a wish. "So, why don't you have children?"

Bettye didn't answer for a moment. She turned her gaze to the window. "Ricky has never wanted children. He always says, 'What do we want kids for? How are we going to raise kids? The world's a mess. We don't even know how to live our own lives, so how could we raise kids?' "

"Maybe he'll change his mind," Andy said softly.

Bettye looked back at her. "No, Andy, I always hoped so, but more and more I've come to realize that we will never have children. Ricky's not going to change his mind, and I wouldn't dare have a child without him saying he wanted it." Her voice wavered with emotion. "You know, I have even grieved over the children I never had. I've had to face the fact that I won't be a mother."

"Well, maybe God has a plan for you that doesn't involve your own children, but involves other children."

Bettye looked at her in surprise. "I hadn't thought of that. I absolutely love little kids. They fascinate me—how their little minds work, their innocence, their trust. I just have such joy when I'm around children."

"Well, there are lots of kids in the world who need adults with that kind of love. Maybe God will give you hundreds of children to love instead of just one or two of your own." Andy reached for her mug of tea and took a long swallow, watchful, letting her words sink in. After a moment she said, "Bettye, have you ever thought of working with orphans or disadvantaged children?"

"No."

"Goodness, Bettye, there are all kinds of things you could do." Andy's voice grew animated. "You could bring kids out here to the farm—city kids who've never ridden a horse, or seen a cow, or gone fishing in a pond, or taken a boat up a river."

"Yes, I could do that, couldn't I?"

"Maybe it's what God wants you to do."

Bettye nodded. Coming from Andy, it all sounded so possible. *Life* seemed possible, imbued with new hope.

"Have you ever prayed about what God wants you to do?" Andy asked.

"No, I . . . I haven't." Bettye cupped her hands around her mug and realized it was no longer warm and comforting. "It's been such a long time since I've prayed about anything."

"How would you feel about getting up early in the morning and having a prayer together?"

"Yeah. I think I would like that. As a matter of fact, Andy, we have cliffs on my farm. Why don't we get up early and go watch the sunrise?"

Andy nodded. "Sounds terrific to me!"

Later, alone in her room, Bettye fell asleep with a sense of hope she hadn't felt in years.

CHAPTER 4

*A*ndy heard an insistent knocking from some distant planet, muffled at first, then loud and intrusive, jolting her from the deep dregs of slumber. She rolled over and pulled the downy comforter up over her head, savoring the cocoon warmth of flannel blankets on a predawn December morning.

The rapping noise sounded again, followed by a remotely familiar voice outside the door. "Andy, wake up! It's me, Bettye. I've got the coffee going. We've got to hurry if we're going to catch the sunrise."

Andy lifted her head and squinted at the bedside clock. Not even 6:00 A.M. yet! She sank back against her pillow and closed her eyes, allowing herself to be lulled back into the pastel haze of a pleasant dream.

"Andy, do you hear me?" That voice again. "Andy!"

"Okay, okay," she groaned, and began the arduous effort of extricating her benumbed body from a blissfully warm bed. *There ought to be a law against getting up before the sun does,* she groused silently as she pulled a sweatshirt over her tangled mop of hair and pulled on sweatpants and boots.

The door opened a crack and Bettye handed her a mug of steaming coffee. "Good morning, Andy. This should help. I'm going to go rev up the jeep. Bring your coffee and come on out when you're ready."

"Okay," she mumbled. That was the extent of her vocabulary at this unearthly hour.

Minutes later, when she stepped out on the rambling front porch and felt the brisk, clean air hit her face, Andy snapped alive. She shivered and pulled up her collar, glad she had worn her warm jacket. Bettye was waiting in the jeep, and the engine was running with a guttural purr. Andy strode across the yard to the driveway and climbed in beside her. It was still too dark to see much. The earth with its rolling pastures and shorn trees looked smudged and shadowy and a trifle surreal.

"I guess you could use a little more shut-eye," said Bettye, looking entirely too pert and chipper for 6:00 A.M. "You're not a morning person, are you?"

"What gave it away?" mumbled Andy, warming her hands on her coffee mug.

Bettye put the jeep in gear and started down the long driveway. "Hope you don't mind this old clunker. It's our farm jeep, a vintage Wagoneer. Dirty, rusty, ugly, and old, but it gets us around the farm."

"That's what counts." Andy swallowed a mouthful of coffee and savored the hot stream warming her innards. Yes, she just might make it after all.

"We'll be taking the back roads," Bettye went on, bright as a tour guide. "By the time we open the gates, close the gates, drive over the fields and along the logging road up through the woods, it'll take us ten minutes to get to the cliffs."

For several minutes the jeep rumbled over a dirt road through dusky, predawn shadows. Suddenly the headlights illuminated several deer crossing the road. One graceful doe stopped and looked their way with a solemn, impervious air, her black eyes incandescent in the stark glare of the jeep's headlights.

Andy held her breath. The doe remained unmoving, staring them down, as if caught in a freeze-frame of time. Then, as swiftly as she had come, she bounded into the brush after the others. Andy thought of the phrase, *holy ground*. This moment in God's lush, untamed wonderland seemed a sign of His presence.

"We always have deer early in the morning," said Bettye.

"Beautiful!" said Andy. "Even though it's dark, I sense the beauty of this place."

"Living here all year, I'm afraid I've taken it for granted," said Bettye, "but you're helping me see it with new eyes." Several minutes down the logging road, Bettye pulled the jeep over and stopped beside a craggy, brush-riddled hillock. "We'll get out here and walk twenty-five feet up the foothills to the edge of the rocks," she told Andy. "The cliffs are two hundred feet up from the river and facing east, so we'll get a wonderful sunrise."

They climbed out of the jeep and trudged together up the rising knoll to the top of the bluff facing the river. They walked to the very edge of the embankment and gazed out over the vast, rolling grasslands. They had arrived at that precise moment in time just before sunrise when the world is silhouetted in shadows and still slightly out of focus, like an old black and white filmstrip.

As they watched, a sliver of dazzling orange sun broke on the horizon, spreading a salmon-pink wash across the sky. One moment there was darkness and shadows, the next, light and color. Andy could see the world coming alive—the Cumberland River flowing below them flanked by groves of trees and the olive-green pastures stretching far off into the distance dotted with grazing cattle.

Andy caught her breath. "It's awesome, Bettye. Do you feel it? Something sacred is taking place here. Think of all the stories in the Bible where something happens on a mountaintop!"

"I feel like . . . like I've just climbed my mountain, thanks to you, Andy. It's almost like a pilgrimage, isn't it?" Bettye walked over to a formation of rocks at the edge of the cliff. "Look, Andy, we have our own little bench."

They sat down on the higher ledge, put their feet on the lower ledge, and faced each other. Andy laughed. "A front-row seat carved just for us!"

"And really quite comfortable." Bettye's voice grew wistful. "I remember the first time Ricky and I saw these cliffs. The first thing he said was, 'This would be a good place to come and pray.' "

"He's right, you know," said Andy. "This is a wonderful place to pray."

Bettye smiled, but there was an urgency in her eyes. "You seem so close to God, Andy. Has it always been that way?"

Andy ran her hand over the cold hard edge of her rock bench. "I believe God had His hand on me from the time I was a little girl. I always wanted to know Him. I wanted to be Joan of Arc, a nun, the whole thing.

"Then, several years ago, I came to the conclusion that something was missing in my life. I couldn't put my finger on it. Finally it dawned on me that I was missing forgiveness and unconditional love. I didn't know what to do about it until one day everything came together in this fast food restaurant in Los Angeles."

Bettye looked baffled. "Fast food restaurant?"

"Yeah. I went to this fast food place in Los Angeles with my girlfriend Deliah—El Pollo Loco. It means 'The Crazy Chicken.' I started telling her how I was feeling, and she pointed right at me and said, 'Andy, did you know that Jesus died for *you*?' And it was like a light went on in my head and I could see the Lord opening His arms to me, and it all just clicked. I thought, *This is it! This is the key! It's Christ's unconditional love and unconditional forgiveness!*

"And I started laughing and crying and saying, 'God, I'm so sorry. I didn't understand. I didn't get it before. I never knew somebody would love me even with all my junk exposed!'"

Bettye studied her. "You seem like someone who always had her life together."

Andy brushed her hair back behind her ear. "Sure, on the outside my life looked great. I was a model, did commercials, had a record deal, a handsome boyfriend. But on the inside, my life was a mess. I thought I had to be perfect to please God; I was always striving, but I still felt guilty, like I could never be good enough.

"But at last I understood that we all fall short. And it's such an equalizer, whether you're a woman of the streets or a sweet little missionary who feels guilty for eating too much chocolate. It's like there's God on one side of the fence, and everybody else is on the other side. And it doesn't matter how close to the fence you stand, you're on the wrong side. And the bottom line is, only Christ can take us over to God's side—and He had to die to do it. That day I knew even if I was the only person, He still would have died for me; He would have forgiven *me*."

Bettye gazed off at the horizon. "It's been years since I've heard anyone talk about Jesus the way you do."

"Were you and Ricky raised in church?"

"Yes. We even walked the aisle and asked Jesus into our hearts. But as teenagers we drifted away. God hasn't been a part of our lives for a very long time."

"He's still there for you, Bettye. His love hasn't changed."

Tears sprang to her eyes. "I know, Andy, I know. As a child, I had faith. God was important to me. I talked to Him all the time." Her blue eyes glistened with unshed tears. "I feel a stirring in my heart, like the memory of a lost love—and I didn't even realize until now that it was gone. How could I have let it go?"

"It's not too late to put your life back into God's hands."

"I want to. What should I do?"

Andy sat forward and took Bettye's hands in hers. "We're going to take everything we talked about last night—your life, your marriage, your future, your fears, everything—and put it all into God's hands."

"I'm so rusty; I don't even know how to pray anymore."

"That's okay. I'll say the words, and you pray in your heart after me."

They finished praying just as the sun burst round and full and red on the horizon, chasing away the final tattered remnants of night. Bettye looked up with tears streaming down her face. As the sun rose, she felt the Son rising within her. She said, "God's back! I feel His presence, Andy. The Holy Spirit is right here. It's as if the *three* of us were holding hands. Thank You, God! Thank You for coming back!"

Andy smiled. "Bettye, He was never gone."

For a while they sat in companionable silence, savoring the serenity and beauty surrounding them. Then Bettye's face clouded. "Andy—what about Ricky? I want him to know God again too. But his heart is like stone. If his heart would just become tender and alive again, maybe God could touch him!"

Andy bowed her head and said, "Dear Lord, Bettye and I come together as sisters. We've committed her life to You, and now she commits her husband to You too. We ask that You change Ricky's heart and make him feel again. Remove the coldness and darkness in his life and fill him with the light of Your Spirit."

When Andy looked up, she saw something new in Bettye's expression—a pure, cleansed innocence in her eyes, an unwavering trust. *She thinks now that we've said this prayer, Ricky's going to come home and everything's going to be perfect in their marriage! But that's not how life is. It may get worse before it gets better. Oh, God, what have I done?*

Andy said levelly, "Bettye, listen to me. This is important. Do you turn Ricky over to God?"

She nodded. "Yes, I do."

Andy squeezed her hand. "Bettye, are you sure? Can you really let go of him?"

Bettye's eyes were gleaming. "Yes, Andy."

"Can you place him in Jesus' hand, no matter what happens?"

Bettye's voice rang with conviction. "Yes, Lord. No matter what happens to us, I turn my husband over to You. I give up, I let go, I surrender. I can't fix my marriage. It's a mess and I just give it all to You."

Andy looked deep in Bettye's eyes and said fervently, "No matter what? Do you trust Jesus to take care of you and Ricky and your marriage? No matter what?"

"Yes, I trust Jesus, no matter what! I give Ricky to God. I give my marriage to God. I give my life to God. No matter what!"

Bettye's tear-streaked face glowed. Her burnished hair was tousled like a child's and framed her porcelain skin with the lucent drama of a cameo. She looked as if she had been touched by angels.

Andy reached over and gave her a spontaneous hug. Even though Bettye was older, Andy felt strangely like the big sister called to watch out for the younger one. She wanted to say, *Hold on, Bettye! It's not all going to be perfect. The commitment you've made may test every ounce of strength you have!*

Another thought struck Andy with stunning impact. *That's what You're asking of me too, isn't it, Lord? To be committed to Bettye, to stand by her and help her, no matter what happens, no matter how long it takes. To stay . . . no matter what it costs.*

No matter what!

CHAPTER 5

*T*hat Sunday morning, after Andy headed back to Nashville, Bettye busied herself around the house, polishing the antique pine baker's cabinet beside the stove, scouring pots and pans and hanging them on the black cast iron rack above the stove, and scrubbing the L-shaped maple counter that divided the kitchen from the dining area. Never mind that the kitchen was already spanking clean. Bettye had to keep busy, or the waiting would be unbearable.

Ricky would be home on Monday and their new life together would begin. Surely he would see that everything was different—that God had touched her in a special way and given her hope. He would see the joy in her face and hear the excitement in her voice and know that God had given their marriage a fresh start.

With every hour that passed, Bettye's anticipation grew. She put a pot of pinto beans to soak overnight— Ricky's favorite meal. She brought in firewood from the porch. She lovingly cleaned each piece of Shawnee cornware pottery Ricky had brought home from his nationwide travels. He had collected so much pottery she had finally told him, "No more!" But they both loved the bright yellow and green colors of the bowls, pitchers, cups, and salt and pepper shakers. The colors were a bold, vivid contrast to the bright red and cobalt blue knick-knacks in the garden window over the sink.

Ricky had always enjoyed these antiques and collectibles as much as she did; and now she wanted him to see their home and possessions with the same eyes of appreciation Andy had given her. That's why it was important that everything look just right.

That night Bettye dreamed of lying in Ricky's arms again the way she had when their love was new and filled with promise. When she woke in the morning she reached instinctively across the bed for him. *He's not here, but he's coming home today, and we'll be together again. God is with us now, and it'll be better than it's ever been!*

Later that morning, with the aroma of simmering pinto beans filling the air, Bettye stood at the window, watching for Ricky's shiny tour bus to rumble up the driveway. She had her makeup just so and her hair styled the way he liked it. She wore a simple brown cotton dress, with a scoop neck and fitted waist that revealed just enough of her figure to be both feminine and mildly provocative. Deep inside, she felt giddy and trembly all at once. It seemed as if Ricky had been gone for years, and now he was coming back to a woman vastly different from the despairing wife he had left behind.

When at last she spotted the huge bus trundling up the gravel road toward the farmhouse, she forced herself to remain calm. She would not rush out; she would remain poised and controlled, waiting. *He's always so exhausted after a tour. Give Ricky his space. Then we'll talk.*

When he's rested and had his supper, then I'll tell him what God has done in my heart, and what He's ready to do for our marriage.

Her heart pounding, she watched Ricky striding toward the porch in his denim jacket and jeans. With his broad shoulders and hard muscular chest, he looked like he could wrestle a heifer with one hand behind his back or pound in a fence post with his bare fist. And yet he possessed a tender, boyish sensuality that melted Bettye's heart whenever she gazed into his russet-green eyes. He wasn't dressed now for an audience or a show. He was just Ricky Shelton, his light brown hair rustling in the wind and curling around his collar, his high cheekbones ruddy with winter's chill, his solid jaw set like a man who knows his own mind and isn't about to change it.

He burst in the door and filled the room with his presence. The whole atmosphere changed in an instant. But whatever Bettye had expected vanished the moment she looked into Ricky's face. He didn't see her; he looked beyond her. He didn't greet her, didn't acknowledge her, simply said, "I've got to go back to Nashville."

She stared at him, bewildered. She wanted to kiss him and feel his smooth cheek against hers, but she knew he would only push her away. This wasn't what she had orchestrated in her mind a thousand times since yesterday morning. "You just got here," she murmured. "Why do you have to go back to Nashville?"

"Radio interview. I'm running late."

"When will you be back?"

"Evening."

"But supper's on—your favorite."

"I'll catch something to eat in town."

SHELTON & LANDIS

He turned and bounded up the stairs. She could hear him up there, walking across the floor from the bedroom to his walk-in closet, then to his bathroom. She could hear a door slam and water running in the shower. He was getting ready for his all-important appointment. She might as well have been invisible or on some other planet.

A half hour later he came treading down the stairs and bolted out the door without a word.

In silence Bettye watched him go. She clenched her fingers and swallowed a sob. *Okay, I'll wait until he comes back. It's not time yet. When he comes back this evening we'll have our time together. It's all right. I'll just wait.*

Bettye ate supper alone. She watched winter's sallow light dissolve into a dusky-mauve twilight. She waited. She cleared her dishes from the table and placed them in the white porcelain sink. She was filling the sink with hot, sudsy water when she heard the front door open. She turned just as Ricky came striding through the kitchen. She smiled and opened her mouth to say, *Hey, welcome home!* But, without a glance her way, he walked past her into the living room.

"How was it?" she called after him.

He didn't answer. He turned on the television and sat down in his recliner.

He didn't even acknowledge me, she thought with a wrenching sensation in the pit of her stomach. *He's been gone for days and he didn't even acknowledge that I'm alive!* She grabbed the dish towel and body-slammed it into the sink. It made a sharp *thwack* sound, but Ricky didn't notice. She marched into the living room and sat down on the couch beside his chair. He kept his eyes fixed on the TV.

S H E   S T A Y S

"Ricky," she said, her voice tremulous, "it's time we talked."

They had had these conversations before. Ricky would get angry and defensive and say, "Don't start on me now. I'm too tired. Don't you add more to my grief!" And she would say, "Something's wrong. We've got to find out what it is." And he'd say, "Not now, not now. Just leave me alone!"

It looked like tonight would be more of the same. Ricky sat staring at the TV, his expression stony, as if he hadn't heard her.

"Ricky," she said more forcefully, "please, we've got to talk!"

His eyes remained on the TV screen. "Good grief, Bettye," he muttered, "I just got off the road. Don't start now. I'm tired."

Bettye sat for a long minute without moving. She could feel her heart pumping inside her rib cage. Her pulse throbbed inside her eardrums. She stood up with a slow deliberation and stepped between Ricky and the television screen. She gazed down at him, waiting.

He heaved a sigh and looked up, his head against the back of the chair, and rolled his eyes at her, as if to say, *Oh, man, here we go again!*

Bettye knelt down in front of him and placed her hands on his knees. She looked up at him and said, "Ricky, I don't deserve this. What's happening here? You've got to talk to me."

He aimed the remote control at the screen and turned off the TV. For the first time in months he looked her in the eye and said, "Okay, Bettye, we'll talk."

Suddenly, a wave of fear washed over her. *Oh, no,*

what's he going to say? No, don't talk! Don't tell me! I don't want to know!

She sat on the floor at his knees. The room was quiet for a long while. No one said a word. Finally, Ricky stood up and started pacing the room. Bettye got up and sat on the couch. She vowed to herself that she wouldn't say a word until he spoke.

The minutes clicked by. They seemed to last forever. Ricky walked back and forth by the stone fireplace and the couch. He walked over to the sliding glass door and stared out into the darkness. He kept pacing, his expression dark and inscrutable. At last he walked over to Bettye and said, "I don't know why I'm not happy. I think I'm dead inside. I haven't had any feeling in me for a long time. I don't feel sad, I don't feel mad, I don't feel hurt, I don't feel angry, I don't feel . . . I don't *feel*!" He looked squarely at her and said quietly, "I don't feel love."

Bettye held her breath. It was as if the earth had stopped moving and the clocks had stopped ticking. She couldn't be sure she would ever breathe again. She waited, listening.

Ricky said, "I don't even feel love for *you*."

Bettye sat very still, her eyes still locked on Ricky's, her lips silent. From somewhere in her head she heard a little girl screaming. The anguished voice was so loud it blocked out everything else; the child was throwing a tantrum, ranting and raving, shrieking at God. *Wait a minute, God! Wait! This isn't the way it's supposed to be! What have You done? I just turned my marriage over to You, I just turned my husband over to You. I just gave everything to You!*

SHE STAYS

It was a shattering, paradoxical moment. On the outside she remained composed, but on the inside she was screaming. It seemed to go on and on, and yet Bettye understood that this was all happening in split seconds. While this little girl screamed at God, Bettye couldn't hear anything else, not Ricky, not even her own thoughts.

Then, for just an instant, the child stopped to take a deep breath as if she were getting ready to scream at God again. And in that moment of silence Bettye heard another voice. Was it Andy speaking to her yesterday on the cliffs? Yes, but it was more. It was God speaking in her heart. She wouldn't have heard His voice over the screaming child's, but in that momentary stillness came the soft whisper, *Do you trust Me?*

And immediately the screaming child shut up.

Bettye sensed that God was waiting for her answer. The screaming child was waiting, Ricky was waiting. The whole world was waiting.

Do you trust Me?

Bettye closed her eyes and whispered to herself, *Yes, Lord, I trust You!* When she opened her eyes, she felt strangely at peace. Even more astonishing, she felt an overwhelming compassion for her husband. She gazed at him, her heart breaking. He had said he had no feelings, but she saw his pain; she saw agony, she saw desperation, she saw grief. She saw the torment in his face and eyes. She thought, *It must have killed him to say that to me!* And she felt the love of Christ for him.

She stood up, went to him, and put her arms around him. She didn't say a word. Just held him. And he put his arms around her. They held each other, engulfed in grief.

60

She began to cry. He began to cry. She had never seen him cry before. All the years she had known him, he had never cried. She could feel the room brimming with their pain.

For a long time they clung to each other. His sobs weren't audible, but she could feel his body shaking and his shoulders heaving. She whispered, "I still love you, Ricky. I'll help you. I'll be there for you. I'll be your friend. We can work through this." She pulled back and saw the tears running down his face.

He broke away from her, strode over to the sliding door, and went outside onto the porch. She remained alone in the room, cradling her arms against her slim body. The words she and Andy had prayed echoed in her memory. *God, turn Ricky's heart from stone to flesh; let him feel!* The idea startled her. *He's feeling now, because he's crying. Thank You, Lord!*

She went over to the door and opened it. The cold night air slapped her face and stung her skin. Softly she asked, "Ricky, what are we going to do?"

He kept his back to her. "I don't know, Bettye. All I know is, it's driving me crazy. I don't know what to do."

"Are you talking about . . . a divorce?"

He pivoted and stared at her. "No, no. I'm not. I don't know what I'm talking about." He came back into the room, his dark eyes desolate. "Bettye, all I know is, I don't feel. It's like everything inside of me is dead. You asked me what's wrong, and I'm telling you. I don't know what I want. I'm not asking for a divorce. I just don't know what to do."

They sat down on opposite ends of the couch. Bettye's mouth felt dry; she was trembling; her body ached as if she had taken a physical beating. She thought, *I've got to help him! He'll lose his mind if he doesn't get this sorted out.* "What are we going to do?" she said aloud. "What do two people do?" When he didn't reply, she asked, "Do you think it's the pressure on the road?"

He held his head in his hands. "No, no. I've been through this before. It's something else."

"Ricky," she ventured, "there isn't anybody else, is there?"

He glared at her. "No, no! There's nobody else! Why would you ask a question like that?"

"I don't know. I guess I'm just . . . I don't know."

"I told you I didn't feel love. If I don't feel love for you, I don't feel love for anybody. I don't *love!*"

She tried another tactic. "Ricky, do you still want to live together?"

His voice sounded ragged, spent. "I don't know, Bettye. I can't stand to be in this house. I just don't know."

"Well, do you want *me* to leave? Or do *you* want to leave?"

He answered with an edge of exasperation. "Let's not do anything right now, okay? Let's just get through the holidays. Let's just wait."

"You mean go home for Christmas like we always do?"

He looked at her as if to say, *Well, of course!*

"Ricky, I don't know if I can."

"Well, we have to. Our families can't know. It'll ruin their Christmas. We've got to go home like nothing's wrong. I've got to work this out by myself. Don't do anything, don't tell anyone."

"Okay, Ricky. We'll go, like always. Like nothing's wrong. I promise."

It was a promise she would come to regret, for that trip home would be harder than she ever imagined.

CHAPTER 6

*B*ettye waited several days until Ricky left home again before telephoning Andy. In a tremulous voice she related the entire story of Ricky's homecoming and their painful confrontation, finally choking out the words, "Andy, he told me he doesn't love me anymore. He won't even sleep in the same bed with me. He's moved to the guest room downstairs. And he's drinking so much. He always has a bottle of beer in his hand. It's like he can't stand to be home without being drunk."

"Oh, Bettye, I'm sorry. I know how much that hurts you. I'm so sorry!"

"I asked if he wanted a divorce. He said he doesn't know."

"Then there's hope, Bettye."

"There's more, Andy. When he was saying he didn't love me and I was feeling so hurt, in my head I heard you asking, *Do you trust God, no matter what?* Only now it was God asking, *Do you trust Me?* And it was so real and vivid, Andy. I said, 'Yes, I trust You, no matter what.' And suddenly His Spirit just filled me with peace. I even told

Ricky I still love him and I'll stand by him no matter how bad it gets."

"Oh, Bettye, you amaze me. You love Ricky in one of the purest ways."

A sob caught in Bettye's throat. "It's not me, Andy. If you hadn't brought me back to God, I would have ranted and raved and thrown things. I would have hated that man with all the vengeance in me. It wasn't me who could love Ricky after he broke my heart; it was the Holy Spirit in me. Thank God you brought me back just in time. If we hadn't prayed together, my marriage would have ended the other night."

"Then, even though you're in separate rooms, you're still together? You're not leaving him?"

"No, Andy. I don't know what Ricky's going through or what's ahead for us. I just know he's in pain, and God wants me to stay."

Andy said softly, "I'm staying, too, Bettye. I'm here whenever you need me. You just call."

"I will, Andy. Listen, I want you to know—Ricky cried."

"He cried?"

"I saw tears running down his cheeks. I held him and felt the sobs heaving in his chest. In all the years I've known him, he has never cried."

"It's a beginning, Bettye. If he's hurting, he's tender enough for the Holy Spirit to work in him. You just let him go. He's in God's hands now."

"I know, Andy. Pray for us. We're going home to Virginia for Christmas. We're not telling our families. We've got to pretend everything's okay. I don't know if I can do it."

"Oh, Bettye, they need to know. Maybe they can help."

"Ricky says no. I'm scared, Andy."

"Bettye, you call me—every day, if you want to. I'm here for you. Actually, I'm moving, but I'll give you my new number."

"You're moving?"

"I'm still flying back and forth to Los Angeles, but I'm also putting down roots here in Nashville. I'm renting a room from Michael Campbell."

"Ricky's ex-manager?"

"Yeah. He's been a good friend to Steve and me. From now on you can reach me either at Steve's or Michael's, or at my L.A. number. Except during Christmas. I'll be in Phoenix a few days at my sister's. Steve's joining me. He's finishing up some work, then flying out. I think it's that project Ricky and Dolly Parton did together."

"You mean the 'Rockin' Years' video," said Bettye. "Have you seen it? It's the most beautiful love song about two people totally committed to each other." She added wistfully, "I just wonder if that'll ever be Ricky and me."

"Don't give up hope, Bettye. God's in control. Trust Him."

"I'm trying, Andy. I told God I'd leave Ricky in His hands. And I want to. But I'm so stressed, I can't think straight. And I've got exams coming up. I told you I'm taking classes at Belmont. And right after Christmas I'm testing out of a personnel management course. How can I study when my whole life's unraveling? Pray for us, Andy. You keep praying."

"I will." Andy paused, then asked guardedly, "Have

you told your friends, Jerry and Linda Thompson, about Ricky?"

Bettye's voice wavered. "Not yet. Linda and I are going on a dinner cruise next Monday on the *General Jackson* showboat in Nashville. I should cancel. I don't feel like partying."

"No, you go, Bettye. Linda's a good friend. Talk to her. If Ricky won't let you tell your folks, you can at least talk to your friends."

"It's going to be hard, so hard, Andy. . . ."

"I know, but Linda cares about you. Go."

"All right, I'll go, Andy. I'll go."

That following Monday, during their drive to the showboat, Bettye confided in Linda about her troubled marriage. Linda didn't seem surprised. With a candidness that unnerved Bettye, she asked, "Is it possible Ricky's seeing other women?"

"No, Linda. Goodness, no! This isn't about other women! If you knew Ricky the way I do, you wouldn't even ask such a thing. Ricky may be confused right now and drinking a little too much, but . . ."

Linda was adamant. "Think about it, Bettye. You admit Ricky hasn't been himself lately. Isn't it possible there's someone else?"

Bettye was feeling annoyed now. "No, Linda, it's not possible. Ricky's not a womanizer. He's the last man in the world who would be unfaithful."

"How can you be so certain, Bettye? Maybe Ricky is—"

Bettye cut her off with a rueful laugh. "You are so off base, Linda. Believe me, that's not our problem. Ricky would never have an affair!"

Linda didn't sound convinced. "Okay, Bettye, if you say so. I won't mention it again." She paused meaningfully. "But, for your own sake, you might consider getting some help."

"What kind of help?"

"Counseling. It wouldn't hurt, and you might feel better if you talked with a professional."

"A professional? You mean a psychiatrist?"

Linda nodded. "I know an excellent one in Nashville."

"I don't need that kind of help. I just need to forget my problems for a while. It's almost Christmas. Let's stop talking about Ricky and have a pleasant evening together, okay?"

But who was she kidding? Already Bettye could feel gloom settling over her spirits. Why did she feel such a need to defend Ricky, even to their closest friends? Was this how the holidays were going to be—constantly trying to justify Ricky when lately nothing he said or did made sense? God help her, how was she going to hold on to her own sanity through this whole ordeal? Maybe Linda was right. Maybe seeing a psychiatrist wasn't such a bad idea after all.

Three days later Bettye had her first appointment with the psychiatrist Linda had recommended. She had to admit she found it helpful to discuss her problems with a trained, objective professional, but she left his office realizing even these visits wouldn't solve her problems. The most she could hope for was that these sessions would help her hone her coping skills for the rough days ahead.

If Bettye had anticipated rough days ahead, the Christmas holidays were at the top of the list. As each day passed, the prospect of maintaining appearances in the intimate confines of the Shelton and Witt households was more than she could bear. Surely Jenks and Eloise would notice how troubled their son was. And what about her parents? Earl and Dorothy Witt had always been good at sensing when one of their six children needed help. Wouldn't they see through this pitiful charade?

As much as Bettye tried to mentally prepare herself to go home and face her family, her fears continued to mount, until one day, in desperation, she telephoned Ricky's mother and suggested they have Christmas at a private fellowship center in Grit instead of at the Shelton home.

"The building is back in the woods and private, yet big enough for everybody. Please, Eloise, let's do this for Ricky," Bettye pleaded, on the verge of tears. "You know how hard it is on him with fans dropping in and people knocking on the door all day long. And the phone rings off the hook. Christmas would be great in the fellowship center. No one would even know we were there." She rushed on, sounding irrational even to herself. "We could decorate and put up a tree and have the wood stove lit so we could cook there. Don't you think it would be perfect?"

Even as the outrageous words tumbled out, Bettye acknowledged privately, *I'll do anything to keep from living our lie in the home Ricky was raised in!*

But Eloise would have none of it. "Bettye, that's the silliest thing I ever heard tell of. We've always had Christmas at my house. That's where it'll be this year and every year as long as I've got life in me."

Bettye hung up the phone with a knot of panic tightening inside her. *We've got to go through this. I'm no actress, but I have no choice. I've got to go home and give the performance of my life!*

So it was settled. They would spend Christmas in Grit with Ricky's parents and in Altavista with hers, and they would do their best to keep their ugly secret from those who had known and loved them all their lives.

Bettye's last hope was that Ricky might reconsider telling their parents the truth. But no. Three days before Christmas, as they packed the automobile for their eight-hour drive to Virginia, he made it clear once more that no one back home was to know their marriage was in trouble.

As Bettye settled into the passenger side of the vehicle, she knew this would likely be her last Christmas with Ricky. They hadn't put it into words, but they both understood that they would separate after the holidays. They would no longer live together under the same roof because Ricky no longer wanted to live in the same house with her. They hadn't discussed which one would leave and which one would stay. The details of their separation seemed unimportant in light of the larger truth that their marriage was in shambles.

They drove in silence over the frigid, snow-packed country roads of Tennessee, Ricky at the wheel, his brow furrowed and his jaw set as he glared straight ahead. Bettye sat with her shoulder pressed against the door, as far from Ricky as the confines of the car permitted. She kept her head turned from him and her eyes remained focused out the side window.

She had her thick personnel management book beside her on the seat. There was so much information to learn before taking her test after Christmas, but she could think of only one thing—the fact that Ricky was making her play the happy couple when they both knew it was a sham. She hated misleading their families. She felt phony, disloyal, dirty.

As they drove she couldn't help remembering happier times. Often when she and Ricky were in the car together, they rode for hours in companionable silence, rarely playing the radio, satisfied just to be together for a quiet ride. Ricky wasn't a big talker; neither was she. So they enjoyed the silence.

But today the silence felt more like a wall between them. It was painful and cutting. It was as if they had already separated and now each had a private battle to face without the other's help. They had this dirty job to do, and nothing could make it palatable.

Bettye felt a dark, mushrooming anger swelling inside her skull. She felt tentacles of bitterness spreading out through her limbs and tightening with an iron grip around her stomach. *Ricky's such a jerk—such a dirty, rotten jerk! How can he be so cruel, asking me to go through this, asking me to put on the biggest act of my life?*

This may be the last Christmas I ever see his parents. I'd have to drop in like somebody who's not family, and say hi for a few minutes and avoid seeing Ricky, and then leave.

That's unfair! I am a family member. Oh, God, I don't want to give up this family. I love this family! I don't want this to be my last Christmas with Ricky's family. Oh, he's such a jerk to take his family away from me!

The anger was erupting into rage, sheer, consuming fury that had nowhere to go; she dared not let it explode

71

or she would lose even this tenuous control over her circumstances.

Help me, Jesus, she prayed silently. *Don't let me wallow in all this self-pity.* And then it struck her. *Look what we did to You. There's nothing Ricky could come close to doing to me that hasn't been done to You, and You kept right on loving us in spite of it all. Help me to love like that.*

The rage dissolved. It was gone. The hatred and bitterness evaporated like mist in the air. Peace flooded back like fresh spring rivers overflowing a dam and cleansing all the dark, hidden crevices of her soul. She felt clean again. The Spirit was once more in charge. Somehow God would see her through these hard days to come.

```
┌─────────────────────────────────────┐
│                                     │
│         C H A P T E R   7           │
│                                     │
└─────────────────────────────────────┘
```

One thing Bettye Shelton could count on. No matter how the rest of the world changed, the rural communities of Grit and Altavista stayed the same, year in, year out. Altavista, with thirty-five hundred people, was the larger town; it was on the map; Grit, with fewer than five hundred families, was not. Altavista, a small, close-knit community where everyone knew everybody else, was an industrial town and home of the Lane Furniture Company. Grit was one long country road with two gas stations, one small market, and seven churches. It had no schools or post office. The two homespun burgs were planted just three miles apart, one on each side of the meandering Staunton River, and shared a stunning view of the majestic Blue Ridge Mountains.

Over the years Bettye had experienced a mixture of feelings when she gazed at the cozy homes and humble storefronts in these rustic, timeworn towns. At times she felt restless, eager to escape their provinciality and insular lifestyles; at other times she returned home broken in spirit and seeking the healing balm of her country roots.

But this trip was like none she had ever made before.

She was coming home wounded, there was no question about that. But she dared not seek the comfort and consolation of family and friends. She must maintain the facade of the blissfully contented wife of one of America's most successful country music stars. And why wouldn't everyone assume she had it made? Didn't the American dream imply that money and fame were the magic combination for happiness? Once she and Ricky had believed the myth as well.

It was evening when Ricky finally turned off Highway 29 and headed toward her parents' home on the outskirts of Altavista. All along Main Street the vintage street lamps were decorated with Christmas lights and holly wreathes. Even the Dairy Freeze, where Bettye and her friends had hung out as teenagers, was decked out for the holidays. The whole town boasted the sweet, cheery nostalgia of a Norman Rockwell painting.

If only Bettye could experience some of that same holiday spirit. She forced a smile, steeling herself to face her parents. The song, "Put on a Happy Face," kept running through her mind. Yes, that's what she was doing. Putting a fake smile in place. Hoping it wouldn't be so brittle it would break. Would her mother see the tears behind her mask? Would her father sense the pain beneath her bright veneer and urge her to confide in him? Surely she wouldn't be able to hide the truth from *them*!

Her mom and dad were two of the wisest, most tender, kind-hearted, God-fearing people she knew. Her father, Earl Witt, Sr., was a jack of all trades—mechanic, carpenter, salesman, heavy-equipment operator, and water-plant supervisor. He could do anything he set his mind to. A World War II veteran, he was from the old

74

school and sometimes lost patience with the way the world was run these days. But he was also a man who wasn't afraid to weep.

His devotion to Dorothy Witt, his bride of nearly fifty years, was admirable. He had nursed her through recent years of ill health, chauffeured her wherever she needed to go, and, during hospital stays, slept in the same room with her so she wouldn't be alone.

Bettye used to dream that she and Ricky would follow the example set by her parents' marriage. Mom and Dad did everything together—gardening, cooking, canning fruit and vegetables, cleaning, shopping, and traveling all over in their camper. Even after all these years Mom still laid out Dad's clothes to put on after his shower.

But Dorothy Witt was more than just a good wife. For over twenty years she worked in a garment factory and still managed to raise six children with a strong work ethic and belief in God. Bettye, the baby of the family, saw her mother as a quiet, patient woman who loved flowers and birds and had a gentle sense of humor. And now that she had grandchildren, she was as devoted to them as she had always been to her husband and children.

Ricky's deep, resonant voice cut into Bettye's nostalgic thoughts. "We're here."

She sat up, her daydreams scattering like confetti. Ricky was pulling into the driveway of her childhood home. It looked the same as always—a little smaller perhaps, and older in the frosty twilight—but familiar and warm and welcoming all the same. There was snow on the roof and in the yard, but her father had shoveled the sidewalks and put rock salt in the driveway to melt the ice. A string of Christmas lights winked from the eaves.

Ricky climbed out and walked around to the trunk for the luggage while Bettye headed for the house. Even before she reached the porch, her father opened the door and emerged with open arms and a generous grin. He looked the same, with his sturdy build, full head of gray hair, and twinkling blue eyes behind his spectacles. Her mother followed close behind him—a striking woman with olive skin, dark brown eyes, and thick, shoulder-length black hair.

They took turns enfolding Bettye in their arms, and then Ricky. Everyone was saying *Merry Christmas!* at once. Bettye noticed Ricky was carrying her suitcase. Hers alone. So! He wasn't planning to stay. She smiled brightly, blinking back tears. She and Ricky stomped snow from their boots and followed her parents inside, exchanging the chill, blustery night air for the heavy, drowsy warmth of the house.

As they shrugged off their overcoats and settled at opposite ends of the couch, the questions started. How was your trip? How are you feeling? What have you been doing? How long are you staying?

It's begun, thought Bettye, keeping her Christmas smile in place. The smile felt stiff and made her jaw ache. As if on cue, she answered every question the way she knew Ricky would want her to.

Her mother asked, "Are you both staying here tonight?"

"No," said Ricky. "Bettye's staying. I'm driving over to Grit."

"You know how we always do it, Mom," Bettye said too quickly. "Our first night in town, I stay here and

Ricky stays with his folks. That way we each get to spend some private time with our families."

Her father nodded. "That's right. It's tomorrow night you two always spend here, so you can wake up together on Christmas morning."

"We'll see," said Ricky, sitting forward restlessly and cracking his knuckles. "I just may stay in Grit."

"Well, everyone will be *here* for Christmas Eve," said her mother. "About forty of us as usual, Bettye—your sister and your four brothers, and all your nieces and nephews. It's going to be a real party, but it wouldn't be Christmas without you here too, Ricky."

He stood up and reached for his coat. "I'll be over. But now I'd better be headin' home." He murmured a restrained good-bye, gave Bettye a dutiful kiss on the cheek, and went striding out the door without a backward glance.

If Bettye had expected her parents to notice an under-current of marital discord between Ricky and herself, she was surprised to see no evidence of concern. Her parents spent the evening talking about the Witt clan's latest trib-ulations and triumphs and catching her up on the latest Altavista news. When the hour grew late, Bettye said good night and headed off to bed. She knew she would need to be well rested to play her big role tomorrow.

By the time Ricky arrived the next evening, the Witt house was already rollicking with the laughter, shouts, and animated conversations of over forty people, half of them children. Bettye was giving her time and attention to the youngsters. She loved hugging them, playing with them, and watching their eyes light up as they gazed at the stacks of bright, foil-wrapped presents under the tree.

While Bettye played games with her little nieces and nephews, she kept her eye on Ricky too. At first he seemed subdued and remote, keeping his distance from the others. But when she noticed him drinking straight shots of tequila, one after another, her alarm turned to anger and indignation. Ricky had drunk beer in front of her parents before, maybe even a mixed drink. But she had never seen him drink straight shots of tequila!

With every drink he became more relaxed and spirited, laughing, telling jokes and swapping stories with the men, and roughhousing with the children. Bettye fumed silently. Didn't anybody notice that he was getting drunk? Or were they too busy having a good time to care? The louder and funnier Ricky got, the quieter and more solemn Bettye grew. She kept thinking, *This could be Ricky's last Christmas with my family, and he's not even going to remember it because he's drunk.*

Later that night, as Bettye watched Ricky drive off into the night, a wave of desolation washed over her. *How can he leave me like this? We've never spent Christmas Eve apart. God help me, is this just the beginning of all the holidays I'll be spending alone?*

She knew Ricky wouldn't go straight home. He would drive around until he was sure his parents had gone to bed. Jenks and Eloise Shelton were good Christian people who would be shocked and dismayed to smell tequila on their son's breath. *Just get him home safe, God,* Bettye prayed silently. *And bring him back safe in the morning.*

Ricky showed up at about 6:00 A.M. to pick Bettye up for the short drive to his parents' house. He looked tired, maybe a little hung over, his expression set like a rock.

78

Neither of them spoke. The idea of talking seemed too exhausting, even to Bettye. They would have enough talking to do when they were with his family.

Even when they were alone in the automobile, they remained silent. Not even a half-hearted *Merry Christmas*. Ricky headed out of Altavista, crossed the narrow bridge over the icy-gray Staunton River, and drove to the top of Jaybird Hill to Grit. It struck Bettye as sadly ironic to be driving along Ricky Van Shelton Boulevard, the street the town had proudly named after their favorite son, Ricky. These days this drive didn't feel like a triumph; it was more like a mockery. It felt like defeat.

They passed Jack Dawson's service station, where hunters and farmers clustered to swap tales of their latest adventures and exploits. As a teenager Ricky had pumped gas at Jack's station. They drove on a few houses down the street to the white, two-story house with the sprawling front porch. Fastened over the porch was the customary five-point Christmas star Ricky loved. Between the pillars, Bettye spotted the old swing Jenks and Eloise always sat in, rocking contentedly and waving at neighbors who drove by. Oh, to go back and live those days again!

But, no. Those days were gone, and this was Christmas morning. She would grit her teeth and do her best to celebrate. Usually she and Ricky were the first to arrive at the Shelton home. Bettye liked to get there by 5:00 A.M., so she could help Eloise prepare her traditional breakfast for the Shelton clan. Today it was nearly 6:30.

Eloise was already in the kitchen kneading the dough for her homemade biscuits. The spicy aroma of sausage baking in the oven gave the house a warm, homey atmosphere. Bettye had always loved the comfy, intimate ambiance of the Shelton home, but now it seemed to mock her, reminding her of all she was about to lose.

"Merry Christmas, Mama Eloise!" As Bettye stepped through the kitchen doorway Eloise broke into a smile and wiped her floury hands on a dishtowel. She was still a fine-looking woman with short, silver hair, fair, wrinkle-free skin, and high cheekbones like Ricky's. A deeply religious woman dedicated to her church, she wore dresses even while gardening and refused to wear makeup or jewelry. She organized yard sales and bake sales for the church and visited the shut-ins and the sick. Eloise Shelton was resourceful, hard-working, and could stretch a dollar farther than any other woman Bettye knew.

She and Bettye embraced. "Well, I wondered when Ricky was going to get you over here! I've got your apron all ready, and I'll just let you crack eggs like you always do."

As Bettye slipped into the cotton apron and tied it around her waist she asked, "Where's Papa Whicker?"—a term of endearment she reserved for Ricky's father.

Eloise always called her husband Whick, a nickname given to him as a child. "Whick's out fetching something in his shop. Can't hardly keep him out of there, even on Christmas day!"

"I heard that, Mrs. Shelton. I guess it's like trying to keep *you* out of the kitchen." Jenks Shelton lumbered into the room in his heavy overcoat, his cheeks ruddy from the cold. He wasn't a tall man, but his frame was solid, if a bit ample around the middle. His brown hair was thinning on top, but the mischievous twinkle in his hazel eyes revealed a wry and youthful spirit. Jenks loved playing pranks and practical jokes; he could tell tall tales like Paul Bunyan, and sometimes he'd get so tickled, tears would roll down his cheeks and his belly would shake like the proverbial bowl full of jelly.

Everyone respected Jenks. A retired factory mechanic who worked part-time at Rose's Discount Store as a general maintenance man, Jenks loved people and was an astute observer of human nature. Yet he took his time forming an opinion about someone and was seldom critical or judgmental. As a committed Christian he had raised his five children with strict discipline and abundant love, earning their admiration and devotion in return. Bettye counted herself as one of Jenks's kids.

The heat from the stove had fogged Jenks's glasses, so he removed them and wiped the lenses with his handkerchief. "Well, Bettye," he said with a grin, "do I get a Christmas hug or not?"

"You sure do, Papa Whicker!" She went into his arms and he gave her a big bear hug. Tears welled in her eyes, but she blinked them back and kept her smile, even though her lower lip quivered.

Jenks said in his booming voice, "All right, Bettye. Now that you're here to crack the eggs, it seems like Christmas."

"I'll do my best to keep out the shells," she said brightly, turning away before he saw her tears.

The radio was on, tuned to the local station. In a smooth, lilting voice, the announcer said, "And, folks, here's our own hometown boy, Ricky Van, singing, 'White Christmas'!"

As Ricky's full, mellow tenor filled the room, Bettye sat down at the table and began cracking eggs into a large Pyrex bowl. In the song Ricky Van Shelton was dreaming of a white Christmas like the ones he used to know.

CHAPTER 8

*B*ettye and Ricky left Virginia the day after Christmas, both of them desperate to give up their dismal charade. Yes, they had pulled it off. No one had suspected they were on the brink of divorce. No one had questioned their motives for leaving so abruptly. But it was a hollow, joyless victory. They drove the eight hours home under the same heavy cloud of silence. Bettye wept quietly; Ricky was closemouthed—until the last few miles.

"You know what we gotta do," he said finally, his voice shattering the silence.

She looked over at him, but he kept his gaze on the road. With a sad note of irony, she said, "You mean, we've got to decide *who's* going to do *what* when we get home?"

"Yeah. We gotta put some distance between us, Bettye. For now, I don't want us living as husband and wife. I can't handle it. I can't be your husband."

She stifled a sob. "I know, Ricky."

"I could find another place."

"Where would you go?"

"I don't know. I guess I could find an apartment."

"No, you can't. It's not practical. You need a place to get your thoughts together. A refuge. Now more than ever before. You're not the kind of person to rent an apartment or live in a hotel. You're a country boy. You need the woods and the dirt roads and the creeks. I know that, Ricky."

"But you're not the one who wants a change, Bettye. It's not fair for me to make you move."

"No, it's not fair," she agreed, "but it's the only thing we can do. You'd go crazy in an apartment. There'd be no peace for you. People would see you come and go. You'd have no privacy." She paused and another thought dawned on her. "You don't want to buy another house, do you?"

He looked at her. "No. This is gonna be a temporary thing. I just gotta get some things resolved in my mind."

"Okay, then I'll find a place in Nashville. I'll rent a place. I don't mind living in the city."

The very next day Bettye drove alone into Nashville and began looking for an apartment. She picked up a rental guide in a supermarket and scanned the listings. She didn't want something cheap and depressing. It would have to be a nice place close to Belmont University.

She spent the day in her car, driving from place to place, five in all. One condominium wanted a one-year lease, but she refused to sign. She didn't want any ties binding her to this new, untried lifestyle.

Another place was unfurnished. She needed a furnished apartment. Something she could walk into with her suitcase and set up housekeeping—a safe haven to step in and out of quickly and easily—a temporary arrangement to accommodate the changing tides of her own unpredictable circumstances.

At the end of the day, just as she was ready to give up her search, Bettye decided to check out one more place—the Village at Vanderbilt. She had avoided Vanderbilt because it had a reputation for being expensive. In her present frame of mind she had no desire for extravagance. But after talking with the manager and viewing the furnished townhouse, she realized this was the perfect spot for her. It was five minutes from the University and in one of the most exclusive areas of downtown Nashville. The utilities were already hooked up and ready to go, and the complex even had a security guard.

It was classy and quiet. The tenants were business and professional people. And it was wonderfully convenient; the complex even furnished linens and maid service. Bettye had to buy only groceries.

With conflicting waves of anxiety and anticipation, she signed a month-to-month rental agreement and paid the manager the deposit. She would move in on January 1, New Year's Day—an appropriate time to begin her new life.

That evening, as she made the one-hour drive back to the farmhouse, Bettye thought about what she had done today. Oddly enough, she felt strong. Driving around Nashville all day with map in hand, she felt she really could do anything she had to do. It was an adventure. It felt good to distance herself from the farm, where she had spent so many months in loneliness and pain.

Something else occurred to her too. *It's possible, Bettye, that you're going to be on your own permanently, not just on a temporary basis. You need to brace yourself.*

If it came to that, she would manage. She had lived alone and supported herself before. She knew she could do it again. But she hated thinking what it would be like not to have a husband. Dating again. Starting a new relationship. It wouldn't be easy giving up the physical side of marriage. *Don't think about it!* she told herself. *Think about becoming a nun, but not about that!*

When she arrived home, Bettye found Ricky stretched out on the couch, nursing a bottle of beer. Empty beer bottles lined the counter tops. "It smells like a brewery in here," she said under her breath.

Ricky looked up and asked, "Did you find a place?"

She sat down in the recliner, suddenly weary, as if the wind had been knocked from her sails. "Yeah, I found a place. I'll be moving in on the first."

He stared at her with a quizzical expression, as if the meaning of her words were finally hitting home. "If you leave, who's going to feed the dogs? Who's going to iron my shirts and water the house plants? What about the bills when they come in?"

She gazed at him for a long minute with a mixture of pity and contempt. He was a spoiled child. He was the very human, flawed, needy, compelling man she loved. "I'll take care of all of it," she said quietly.

"How are you going to do that in Nashville?"

"I'll come home when you're not here, and I'll take care of everything like I've always done. And when you are here, I'll stay in town." She wanted to say more. *Don't you understand, Ricky? You're still my husband and this is still my home, and I wouldn't dream of letting go of my responsibilities. The only reason I'm leaving is in hopes that you'll get your head together and realize you want our marriage to work.*

She looked at him as he took another swig from his bottle and knew he wasn't ready to hear how she really felt. Her words would roll off him like rainwater on an oil slick. A sudden melancholy darkened her spirits. *There are two people sitting here together, but there's no communication. I'd rather there not be the two of us if it means feeling so alone with him.* Impulsively she reached for his bottle. "Give me some. You like it so well."

He handed her the bottle and she swallowed several mouthfuls, too quickly. It burned going down. A small voice somewhere in her head said, *Don't do this! You've just rededicated your life to Christ. Don't quench the Spirit within you.*

Silently she argued back, *I'll do whatever it takes to get Ricky to open up and talk to me and maybe even be with me as his wife again. If it means getting drunk with him, that's what I'll do!*

Ricky reached toward her. "Give me back my bottle."

She moved over to the couch beside him and held the bottle out of his grasp. She smiled invitingly. "If you want it, Ricky, you get it."

He reached across her and clasped her wrist. "Come on, Bettye. Stop teasing. Get your own beer."

She took another swallow and handed it back to him. He finished off the bottle, got up, and went to the kitchen. He was back a minute later with two open bottles. He plopped down beside her and handed her one. "Now you've got your own."

She snuggled against him. "I don't want mine; I want yours."

He laughed and pushed her away, and she pushed him back, as if they were roughhousing children. They drank for a while in silence. Bettye could feel the alcohol numbing her senses and blurring the world into a rosy haze. She felt mellow. She put her head back on Ricky's shoulder and closed her eyes. "Ricky," she murmured, "how are you feeling?"

He chuckled. "I ain't feelin' no pain, Bettye."

"You feeling real good?"

"I'm feelin' real good."

"You wanna feel even better, Ricky?" She nuzzled his neck. "You wanna go upstairs and lie down?"

He nodded drowsily. "Yeah, I'm tired. I wanna go lie down." He heaved himself up off the couch and stumbled down the hall. Bettye watched with a stab of disappointment. He wasn't going upstairs to her bed. He was heading for the downstairs guest room, where he had been sleeping for the past several months.

She followed him. It was a pleasant room with an antique pinewood armoire, pine dresser and mirror, and a Persian rug on the off-white carpeted floor. Patchwork quilts made by Ricky's fans were stacked on an oversized antique trunk, and a white carousel horse stood in the corner beside a child's rocking chair.

Ricky pulled back the covers and climbed into the four-poster bed. Bettye crawled in beside him. He pushed her away. "You go get in your bed, Bettye. I don't want you to sleep with me."

The words stung like darts. Like a child rebuked for displeasing her elders, Bettye got out of bed and tramped out into the hallway. She stood trembling, cradling her arms, wincing as if she'd been physically wounded. He

_88_

didn't want her. Even drunk, he didn't want her. The alcohol's numbing anesthesia was wearing off. The pain was back, worse than before.

With the pain came a new resolve. *I'm not going to give up that easy!* She turned back to the bedroom. The door was shut. She turned the knob. It was locked. "Ricky," she called, "I want to talk to you. Open the door!"

His muffled voice came back, "No, Bettye. I'm tired. Go to bed. I don't want to talk."

She rattled the handle. "Ricky, open the door. I really need to talk to you. Don't lock me out!"

"Bettye, I'm tired and I'm drunk and I just want to sleep. Now go to bed. We'll talk in the morning."

She seized the knob again. Fury shot through her like wildfire. She shook the door. "Ricky, don't lock me out. Please don't lock me out!"

"Go to bed, Bettye!"

Her voice rose shrilly. "Ricky, open the door!" She was begging now. "Ricky, please open the door. Please, Ricky!"

"Bettye, go to sleep."

She began to sob. "Ricky, please, I just want inside. If you'll just open the door and let me inside. Don't lock me out, Ricky. Don't lock me out!"

He didn't answer. She jiggled the handle again and waited. Still no answer.

Her mind raced. *What can I do to open this door?* An idea came to her. She ran down the hall to the wash room and rummaged through Ricky's tool box. Ah, this was it. Her fingers closed around the solid wood handle of a hammer. Raising it like a tomahawk, she charged back

89

down the hall to the guest room. With all her strength she slammed the hammerhead against the door. All the doors in the hallway ricocheted with the impact and Ricky's dozens of gold and platinum albums rattled against the wall. It sounded like a gunshot.

"Ricky, open this door!" she shouted, and took another swing. This time the hammer hit the doorknob head on. She could feel the repercussion boomerang up through her arms. She swung again, her momentum growing, her rage taking on a life of its own. "Ricky, open the door!" she screamed.

She kept swinging, battering the door in a blind frenzy. The wood began to splinter and paint chips flew up like feathers. Bettye couldn't stop. Part of her was out of control, but another part watched in pleased fascination.

At last one surging blow hit its mark and the door crashed open, slamming against the wall with a thundering explosion. The whole room shook. Bettye marched in with the hammer still in her raised hand and glared down at Ricky. He lay in the bed, his eyes big as saucers, his face blanched white as the sheet.

She threw the hammer on the floor and nailed Ricky with her gaze. Releasing every word with the stinging precision of an arrow, she warned, "Ricky Van Shelton, don't you *ever* lock me out again!"

Before he could utter a sound, she turned on her heel, stomped out of the room, and went upstairs to bed.

When Bettye woke the next morning, the house was quiet. She got up, pulled on her jeans and a sweat shirt, and headed downstairs. She went to the guest room, but the bed was empty, the covers tossed aside, the pillow and mattress still showing the impression where Ricky had lain.

She gazed at the splintered door. Paint chips were scattered over the floor like snow flurries. The doorknob lay broken in two pieces, several feet apart.

Had she done this?

Me and my little hammer, she acknowledged with a stab of regret. But where was Ricky? Had he left for good, convinced she was a madwoman?

She ran to the front window and looked out. Thank God, Ricky was there, moseying along the driveway, dressed in a rumpled leather jacket, faded jeans, his baseball cap, and favorite work boots. He was too far away for her to read his expression. Was he angry? Did he hate her? Would he give her a piece of his mind or avoid her altogether?

She slipped out on the porch. She had to face him. No use putting it off. With head lowered, she trudged down the steps and shuffled out to the driveway. With every step she felt her face burning hotter with shame.

From the end of the driveway Ricky spotted her and stopped. He stood waiting, watching her, the brim of his hat casting a shadow over his face. She kept walking, slowly, reluctantly, each step harder than the one before. He didn't move. Just waited and watched.

It was the longest walk of her life.

When she reached him, she looked up into his face.

He was grinning.

She lowered her head and mumbled contritely, "Ricky, do you think you could fix my door?"

He burst out laughing. "You were coming through that door, hell or high water, weren't you?"

She met his gaze. "I don't know what came over me, Ricky. All I knew is there couldn't be a locked door between us. You didn't give me any choice. I had to unlock the door."

He was still chuckling. "Yeah, I can fix the door, Bettye. Don't worry, I can fix it."

CHAPTER 9

*A*ndy Landis felt uneasy. Even a trifle panicky. These days it seemed she was constantly asking herself, *Girl, what on earth are you doing now?*

At the moment she was driving over slick, snow-clogged streets to Bettye Shelton's new townhouse in the icy heart of Nashville. The temperature was below freezing, and Andy felt an icy dread settling over her own heart.

It had been over a month since she and Bettye had prayed together on the cliffs, and since that time things had gone from bad to worse. Bettye's marriage had crumbled; she and Ricky had separated and were on the verge of divorce; and now Bettye had moved into her own place.

It wasn't supposed to have worked out this way. Andy had been so certain that God had sent her to the Shelton farm to help Bettye and Ricky.

Way to go, Andy! she chided herself. *You've sure got a funny way of helping! Keep it up and you won't have any friends left! At least, no happily married friends!*

Through her frequent phone calls, Bettye had kept

Andy informed of the painful disintegration of her marriage, even calling over the holidays with private updates from Jenks and Eloise Shelton's house in Grit, Virginia. Every call proved more disheartening than the one before.

But other sources were bringing Andy even more disturbing news. Rumors were circulating throughout the country music industry that Ricky Van Shelton was in trouble. He was drinking too much. Partying too hard. The fact that his marriage was on the rocks was only the tip of the iceberg.

People who knew that Andy was close to Bettye had started watching what they said about the Sheltons. Or they would tell Andy, "You've been around. You know what happens. Marriages come and go in the entertainment business. So why waste your time worrying about Ricky Van's marriage?"

Andy found herself thinking, *How do I tell these people who don't believe in God that God told me to do this?* Usually she ended up saying, "I'm just doing what I would want somebody to do for me."

And now Andy was on her way to Bettye's townhouse to face her for the first time since their morning on the cliffs. No matter how it played, it was going to be an awkward reunion. Andy could imagine herself saying, *Well, Bettye, now that I've ruined your life and you've moved out of your house, what would you like to talk about?*

Did Bettye blame Andy for her marital troubles? Had she invited her over just to be polite? Was Bettye just waiting to tell Andy what she really thought about her meddling in her life?

Andy pulled into the parking area of the Village at

Vanderbilt and gazed at the rows of attractive two-story apartments with slate-gray siding and red-brick trim. Wouldn't you know, there wasn't a place to park. She drove around twice and finally found a spot a good distance from the townhomes.

Before stepping out of her car, she buttoned her long black coat and tied her scarf around her neck. Now if she could just navigate from her car through the maze of apartments without slipping on the ice and breaking her neck.

As she crunched gingerly through the snow, making her way to the glistening sidewalk, the wind stirred and whipped against her face. The cold snatched her breath momentarily. It was going to be a long, bleak walk. Now which place was Bettye's? Did she say the one on the right or the one on the left?

Oh, Lord, I must be insane! Andy groaned inwardly. *What am I doing here? I haven't seen this woman in weeks. What makes me think she'll even want to see me again? How do I know I won't make things worse than they already are?*

Andy finally found the correct address—sure enough, the condo on the left. A pizza delivery man was just leaving Bettye's place and coming down the sidewalk toward her. His cheeks and nose were ruddy and his face looked pinched from the cold.

Andy chuckled to herself. *He doesn't look any happier about braving this weather than I am. What's that saying? Neither rain, nor sleet, nor ice, nor snow . . . no, that's the mailman.*

She climbed the steps to the small porch and knocked on the door. *Help me, Lord,* she prayed silently. *I'm com-*

SHE STAYS

ing here to cheer up Bettye, and right now I'm a little short on that commodity myself.

But the moment the door opened, Andy's uncertainties vanished. Bettye stood there looking small and young and sad and weary. She looked needy and fragile, like a young girl who's been knocked down and is waiting for someone to help her up. Andy's protective feelings flooded back. *I was right. I've got to stand strong for her. I have to be the big sister.*

Bettye smiled and her blue eyes shone. "Bless your heart, Andy, don't stand out there freezing. Come on in!"

Andy stepped into the warm apartment and the two women embraced.

"You look great in that coat," said Bettye.

"Thanks. I love it. I got it in Ireland. Usually the weather's not cold enough to wear it, but today—"

"I know. The wind chill factor must be ten below."

While Bettye hung up her coat, Andy glanced around the room. Thin wintry sunlight streamed in through the enormous front windows and sliding glass doors. All the walls were off-white and bare, except for an occasional neatly framed print. The furniture was tasteful and attractive—a modern decor Andy couldn't quite place. French provincial perhaps.

Andy could imagine every apartment in the complex containing this same melange of furniture, perhaps in different color combinations, but every table and lamp and chair would be placed just as these were, with the sterile, impersonal perfection of a physician's waiting room.

Andy wondered if tenants were allowed to rearrange things. Would these rooms ever possess the casual, congenial clutter of a real home? Or did Bettye choose this place because of its very detached, impersonal quality?

One could live here and remain dispassionate and uninvolved. It was a safety zone. Bettye could come here, be replenished, and walk away without feeling she had left a piece of herself behind.

"I like your place," said Andy. "It's wonderful. So clean and cozy. And there's so much light."

"That's what I like about it too," said Bettye. "It needs a few touches to make it feel like home, but it's got everything I need." She gestured toward the stairs. "There are two bedrooms and a bathroom upstairs. I asked the manager if I could use one bedroom as an office for studying, and she called the furniture company right away and had them exchange the bedroom suite for office furniture. It was great. I thought, 'Oh, Lord, You've taken care of everything! What else could I possibly ask for?' "

Andy's eyes filled with unexpected tears. "You still feel that way, Bettye, after all that's happened? You feel God has given you everything you've asked for?"

Bettye's voice wavered. "Maybe not yet, but I'm trying to do what you said, Andy. I truly want to put my husband in God's hands and trust the Lord, no matter what."

Andy's spirits lifted. Her instincts were correct. This was where God wanted her! A smile spread across her face. "Bettye, I know God's called us together to pray for your marriage and your husband. We're going to bombard heaven with our prayers. The angels are going to know our prayers by heart before we're through."

Bettye smiled tentatively. "Before we pray, Andy—shouldn't we eat our pizza? Before it gets cold?"

"What kind is it?"

"Double cheese and pepperoni."

"Do you have any cracked red pepper?"

"No, I don't have anything here, Andy. Just pizza."

Andy laughed. "Well, by all means, let's eat! I think the Lord will understand. He wouldn't like cold pizza either."

Bettye's smile deepened. "I'm so glad you're here, Andy. You just don't know!" Her eyes glistened and her skin shone like alabaster. She didn't look quite so small and sad and helpless anymore; in fact, she looked positively radiant.

As they sat at the kitchen table eating pizza and drinking sparkling water Andy asked about Ricky. "Is he at home or out on tour?"

"On tour again. He always faxes me his schedule, so I know where to reach him. But it's just as well he's away. Things were deteriorating rapidly at home." In a halting, mortified voice, Bettye told Andy about the incident with the guest room door. "I couldn't believe I did such a thing. It's not like me at all. It must have been the beer. I knew it was wrong, but I thought maybe I could win him back if I drank right along with him."

"It doesn't work, does it—doing something that makes you feel bad about yourself just to please someone else?"

"No, it really backfired. What a disaster!"

Andy stifled a grin. "I sure wish I could have seen Ricky's face when you broke in with that hammer."

"Well, Ricky knows I'll never allow a locked door be-

98

tween us again." Bettye paused, her blue eyes darkening. "But there's so much distance between us now, so much more than a locked door."

"Are you still going back to the farmhouse?"

"Only when Ricky's not there. I go back to clean and feed the animals and pay the bills. It's still my home, Andy."

Andy shook her head in wonderment. "Goodness, Bettye, I don't think I could do what you're doing."

Bettye shrugged. "What else can I do? Someone has to take care of things when Ricky's not there. And no one knows we've separated."

"Your family doesn't know you're living here in Nashville?"

"Yes, they know that much. I told them the truth as far as it goes. I said I feel a sense of urgency to finish my college degree, so this semester I'm going to the university full time. I told them the long commute from the farm is too hard during these winter months with the bad weather and all. And I told them I was afraid to be driving back and forth at night. All that's true. And, of course, with Ricky on the road so much, it made sense for me to rent a house in town."

"What did your family say?"

Bettye smiled grimly. "They thought it was a stroke of genius. They said it was great that we're so successful we can afford both a townhouse and a country home."

"It must be hard not being able to share your heart with the people who love you."

Bettye's eyes moistened. "It is. Sometimes I just want to tell them the whole story. But then I stop myself, because I know it would be even harder if they knew."

"Well, you can talk to me," said Andy. "I'll listen all you want, and then we'll pray."

"I don't even know where to begin. It's just so hard, Andy. I don't know where Ricky's head's at anymore. I just know he's hurting."

Andy reached across the table and touched Bettye's hand. "Listen, Bettye, here's what I think. We need to *not* talk about Ricky. We need to *pray* for Ricky and talk about *you*."

"Okay, Andy. But I warn you, there's not all that much to say about me."

"Sure, there is. I want to hear about your family, and how it was for you growing up, and what you were like as a little girl. What did you dream about? What did you want to be?"

Bettye smiled. "Okay, but remember, it was your idea."

Andy leaned forward, her elbows on the table. "And, Bettye, be thinking about what it is *you* want. You're not just Ricky's wife; you're Bettye! This is your world now. You can do things your way. It's not just what Ricky wants. It's what you want, what you think, what you need."

"It's hard for me to think like that, Andy. All my life I've felt like I should be making other people happy."

"Listen, girl, it's time to think about what makes *you* happy. That's part of knowing who you are inside. It's part of becoming a whole, healthy person that God can use."

"You know, Andy, you're making me feel better already."

Andy glanced around at the snug little kitchen. "Bettye, I sense something. The Holy Spirit's going to do a work in you here. It's going to be a special time. This is a place where you can rest and heal."

Bettye followed her gaze. "Do you think so? I know it's where I should be for now, but I . . . I'm already lonely."

"Well, I see this as your haven. It's almost like a sanctuary."

Bettye brightened. "I like that, Andy. My sanctuary."

"And right now we're going to pray for the angels to fill up this place and protect you and comfort you."

"Yes! You pray, Andy. You say the words."

Andy gripped Bettye's hand across the table. "Heavenly Father, God, thank You for giving Bettye this place. We know it's going to be her sanctuary where You can come and speak to her and heal her pain.

"Lord, I know You love Bettye and Ricky. You love Ricky even more than Bettye does. We've placed him in Your hands. We know You have a plan for him that's better than anything Bettye could even dream of. You want him to be Your child. We ask You to take our hands away; take Bettye's hands off Ricky if she tries to hold on to him. As hard as it is, we surrender him to You. Father, remind us when we forget that no one truly belongs to us; they belong to You. Bettye belongs to You.

"And because You say where two or three are gathered in Your name You will be with them, Bettye and I join together in asking You to surround this house with angels dressed all in white and carrying great flames of protection. Let them make a hedgerow around Bettye and block every window and door. Protect her from every side so nothing bad can pierce her heart. Make this little condominium a sacred place.

"May everything we say and do help us to heal and grow and mature to become the women You want us to be. Lord, I'm honored that You've called me to Bettye. Use me only for her good. In Jesus' name, amen."

When Andy opened her eyes, she saw tears rolling down Bettye's cheeks. Her own throat felt tight with unshed tears. Bettye looked around with a light of expectation on her face.

"What is it?" asked Andy.

"Don't you feel it?" said Bettye. "It's happening. I know it is. Don't you feel them? This whole house is filling up with angels!"

CHAPTER 10

*I*n January 1991, as the Persian Gulf crisis worsened and the United States prepared to attack Iraq, Bettye Shelton was settling into her new life in Nashville. While the world collectively held its breath to see what the future would bring, Bettye pondered her own uncertain future. With newscasts predicting war and with anxiety gripping the nation, Bettye was fighting her own war of anxieties—and she was winning!

She was daring to hope again.

Every day Bettye's heart grew more attuned to the Holy Spirit within her. He was her constant companion. No longer was she listening just to the sound of her own voice; no longer did she feel alone and abandoned. She sensed His presence, the way a blind person must sense someone else in the room even when there isn't a sound. Knowing that God loved her enough to give His Spirit to commune with her changed everything. Every day she discovered new ways He was transforming her.

He had changed her attitude about the townhouse. At first she had seen it as a painful symbol of her broken marriage; she grieved over having to leave her home with

Ricky to live in this strange new place, alone. But now she also saw her townhouse as an opportunity for growth, a proving ground for her faith, a place where she could become the whole person God wanted her to be. Even though she no longer had the protective umbrella of a loving husband, God was providing for her in every way —mentally, emotionally, spiritually, and physically.

Her classes at Belmont provided plenty of mental stimulation. Her communications class gave insights into the dynamics of relationships, including hers and Ricky's; stress management class helped her deal with her own stress; New Testament history pushed her to explore the truths of the Scriptures; and aerobics helped her improve her self-image and get back in shape physically.

Once a week Bettye visited her psychiatrist, a Christian man who encouraged her to express her feelings and look for ways to cope with the crises in her life. Often he assured her, "Bettye, you're not crazy. You don't need to see me. You're one of the sanest people I've ever known. But if you want to figure out what Ricky is going through, I can help you understand what might prompt him to behave the way he is."

Bettye's faith deepened as she spent precious hours in the Word and in soul-stirring prayer with Andy. It was astonishing, the way God was engulfing Bettye with His goodness. How could she indulge in self-pity or despair when He was meeting her needs in so many ways?

For some time Bettye had been seeing a chiropractor for treatment of lower back pains. When he suggested she see a physical therapist, she began therapy twice a week. During her first visit, the therapist asked, "Exactly what kind of exercise are you involved in?"

"None."

"Well, let me put it this way. What kind of sports do you participate in?"

"None."

"Well, okay, what is it you do for fun?"

Bettye thought hard for a minute. *What do I do for fun? Goodness, what is it I do for fun?*

He said, "Well, maybe, uh, do you play tennis?"

"No."

"Probably golf."

"No."

"Hiking?"

"No."

"Waterskiing? Snowskiing?"

"No."

"Bowling?"

"No."

She could see him backing up a little in his chair, and the pitch of his voice rose slightly. He was obviously grasping for straws. "Maybe you go mountain climbing?"

"No. I'm sorry."

"Or roller blading, or skating, or—?"

"Do you mean grown people actually do these things?" she asked in amazement.

His shoulders dropped perceptibly. "Mrs. Shelton—Bettye—is there anything you do for fun?"

She was silent. It was a sad, almost comical moment. "You know, I don't think so." The realization sank in. She had not had fun in a very long time. "I've never even owned a bicycle or learned how to roller skate," she admitted sheepishly.

The therapist sat forward and smiled. "Well, we're going to change all that."

He worked with her for several weeks until her back was stronger, keeping her to a strict regimen on the exercise equipment, then giving her relaxing massages to loosen tense muscles.

One day he approached her with knee pads, elbow pads, gloves, and a helmet, and said, "We're going to do something different today. We're going to roller blade."

Before she could protest, he strapped the helmet on her head. Once upright on the skates, she wobbled and lurched along like a klutz, embarrassed to have her therapist—a perfect physical specimen—see how clumsy and uncoordinated she was. As he urged her to try her wings —or *blades*—she clung to him for dear life, laughing and crying at once. "Don't let go of me, please don't let go of me!"

For several sessions he skated with her, guiding her, steadying her, helping her up when she fell down, and always, always cheering her on. Finally he told her she was ready to solo. And she did, she actually did! Roller blading alone, she felt a taste of the freedom and grace of an eagle in flight; it was an exhilarating, liberating, delicious, carefree glide! Once she gained confidence, she enjoyed her afternoons roller blading with her therapist. She sensed God working through this platonic relationship to meet her need for harmless physical contact with a man.

As Bettye established a separate life from Ricky, she marveled that God had freed her even from financial worries. While packing to move out of the farmhouse, she had overheard Ricky's business manager asking, "Do we need to take Bettye's name off the checking accounts?"

SHELTON & LANDIS

Bettye understood why he asked the question. It was his job to protect Ricky's assets.

But Ricky replied, "No, give her anything she wants. It's business as usual. Bettye signs all the checks. She's got the VISA card. Anything she wants, you give it to her."

It was God's way of saying, *All you need is My safety net; listen to Me; follow My instructions; hang in there, and you'll be okay!*

Bettye was convinced. She was feeling stronger, more at peace with herself, with her life, and with God. She decided it was time to confide in her friends about her marital separation. She needed their support. First, she told Ricky what she planned to do. He didn't argue. So one evening she invited Rick and Carolyn Kitts and Jerry and Aleta Daugherty over to her townhouse and told them the truth.

They responded as she knew they would—with shock, anger, and disbelief. Rick Kitts told her, "I swear, Bettye, I think I need to take Ricky out and beat some sense into him. You just tell me, and I'll go beat the daylights out of him!"

"No, Rick," she protested. "We're talking about Ricky here. He's suffering right now. But he's a good man. You know he's a good man. We've got to believe that goodness is still there deep down inside him."

Bettye's unswerving belief in Ricky had helped to see her through those first trying weeks of January as she ate alone in her tiny kitchen, gazed at blank walls, or walked daydreaming among oaks, maples, and willows on the lush Vanderbilt campus. She sensed a peace, a permanence in these surroundings that fed her need for continuity and stability. She felt invigorated watching students strolling arm in arm, or chatting together on the lawn, or standing by easels sketching the graceful, time-worn buildings. In spite of her own upheaval, other lives were moving on with a sweet, ordinary sameness. She could count on that, and it was somehow reassuring.

The next time Andy came to visit, Bettye met her with a new buoyancy of spirit. She told Andy about her classes, the helpful sessions with her psychiatrist and physical therapist, and the poignant visit with her friends to confide the news of her separation. She concluded with a hint of mystery in her voice. "You won't believe what I'm doing now, Andy. I've learned to roller blade, and I'm not too bad."

Andy laughed with delight. "You never cease to amaze me! I can just see you skimming along the sidewalks like a teenager. What will you think of next?"

"I don't know, but I've got our old standby for tonight. Pizza with pepperoni. It was just delivered."

Andy's eyes twinkled. "Did you remember the cracked red pepper?"

"Oh, Andy, I'm sorry. But I tossed us a salad."

"Salad will do."

As they ate, Bettye asked, "What about you, Andy? What's happening in your life these days?"

Between mouthfuls of pizza, Andy replied, "Aside from a little flare-up of my endometriosis, I'm great. Busy writing songs for Warner/Chappell. I also started writing for a Christian company, Star Song. I'm working with Dwight Liles, a terrific guy. We talk about our faith. I told him I learned about God by trial and error, through pain, from the Word, and by faith. Some people put God in a box, but we believe you should just blow the doors off that box and let God be God."

"I'm learning that lesson myself," said Bettye with a smile.

After eating, they settled in the living room, Bettye on the sofa, Andy in the wing chair. They were both comfortable in their usual attire—sweaters, jeans, and no makeup.

"I think God is starting to heal me," said Bettye as she traced the tufted arm of her sofa. "I'm getting better with your help, Andy."

"Maybe it's time for an even more radical step of faith."

"Like what?"

"Like maybe facing some important truths about who you are and what you were like growing up. If you're game, I brought some music to set the mood. Guitar and piano, with birds singing, and waterfalls in the background."

"Okay, why not?"

Andy went over to the stereo and put on a cassette tape. Bettye watched Andy intently. She realized that she had developed a deep trust and respect for her. Andy was so full of love, joy, and expectancy in spite of a lifetime of trials that would have crushed a less resilient soul. She had been sexually molested as a child and raped as a young adult. She'd overcome severe cervical dysplasia, chronic fatigue syndrome, abuse, and deafness. Yet there was no sign of bitterness or defeat in her eyes. In fact, Andy was one of the most joyful people Bettye had ever known. Yes, Bettye was more than willing to share her past with this courageous woman.

As the music filled the air, Andy said quietly, "Bettye, I feel like there's still part of you that's hurting, a part of your past you need to get in touch with. Tell me, what were you like as a little girl?"

Bettye smiled. "I was the baby in the family, and I loved being Daddy's little girl and having my four brothers dote over me."

"Can you picture yourself when you were maybe four or five years old?"

Bettye grew thoughtful. "Yeah, I was a little girl with long brown curls. They were a bit frizzy, but they made perfect locks. And, uh, I had a chubby little face."

"Tell me about the girl—a favorite memory. Describe it as if you're watching a movie."

Bettye was silent for a minute. Finally she said, "The girl is putting on a little wedding dress for a Tom Thumb wedding, and she's the bride."

"Is she pretty?"

"Yeah, I guess she's kinda pretty. She's beaming, because she's the center of attention. People are taking pictures of her and asking if they can have a lock of her beautiful hair. She doesn't want anyone else to have a lock except her daddy, so she cuts off the lock and gives it to him. But it makes him unhappy. He doesn't understand why she would cut her hair like that."

"So she didn't always please her dad?"

"She tried to, but she couldn't always."

"Bettye, how did she feel when he wasn't pleased?"

"Devastated." Her voice quavered. "It broke my heart when I made my daddy upset. All he had to do was give me a long, disappointed look and my heart broke."

"Bettye, what happened when you were older? It

110

SHELTON & LANDIS

might help you to remember the different parts of yourself you've left behind. The girl you were at five, and at twelve, and at seventeen, and twenty-two."

"Why, Andy? The teenage girl became rebellious. She felt terribly unloved and rejected. But that's all in the past."

"No, Bettye, it's not. It's all part of who you are now." Andy sat forward and her voice grew gentle. "I believe when a lot of us get saved we cut off all the stuff that happened before; it's like we're saved from here forward. But God is omnipotent. God is omnipresent. When He heals us, He's not just healing us from today forward; He's healing us from today back too. He heals our yesterdays as if they were today, because there's no yesterday for Him.

"So, Bettye, go back again to when you were five. You're this wonderful little child with curly, frizzy hair. You deserve to be loved, not because you're so good, but because God made you. He created you to be loved. He made you lovable. Don't you see? You've forgotten that He made you this precious, innocent child who laughed and played and was happy and had dreams. Think about that five-year-old girl again. She's still a part of you. Picture yourself standing alone in a room, and Jesus comes in. Can you see Him, Bettye?"

"Yes, I see Him."

"Can you describe Him?"

"He's wearing a white robe, and He's smiling. He comes in and He sits down."

"What does He say to you?"

Bettye began to weep softly. "He says, 'I love you.' "

"And what do you do?"

S H E   S T A Y S

The sobs came harder. "I run and climb up in His lap."

"And what is He doing now, Bettye?"

"He's holding my hand. He's holding me in His arms like a daddy holds his little girl."

"And how do you feel?"

"I feel warm and safe. I feel loved and accepted. I know He'll always be there for me. He'll always love me, no matter what. I'll always be His little girl."

"Now, Bettye, can you see Jesus loving the young girl at twelve, and at seventeen, and twenty-two? Can you see Him accepting not just the woman you are today but the person you've been at every age? He's accepting *you*, Bettye. He loves *you*, all that you've ever been and ever will be. Can you imagine how love like that feels?"

Bettye looked at Andy, marveling. "That's the way it's supposed to be, isn't it? God loves me so much He wants me to be the person He made me. That pleases Him."

"What are you thinking now, Bettye?"

"I'm thinking I've had it all wrong. I've lived my whole life wanting to please all the men in my home, and God never asked me to do that. Ever since I can remember, I needed to be cute and charming for my daddy and my brothers. I felt if I wasn't cute enough, they wouldn't like me.

"I saw my mother and sister doing the same thing. It was just the role we took on. No one asked us to. We just figured we were supposed to please the men. It seemed like the only way I could be happy was to make sure someone else was happy."

Bettye straightened. She felt the blood pumping faster

in her veins; her senses were heightened, so that every note from the stereo sounded in her head and every beam of lamplight glared behind her eyes. "Oh, Andy, I've brought that feeling right with me into adulthood, haven't I—with my male teachers and the men I worked for? I beat my head against the wall to do everything perfect, so they'd never be displeased with me. I made *As* in school; I worked overtime. All of it!

"And Ricky! All the years we've been together, I've felt the need to please him at any cost. I was losing myself trying to please him. And when he rejected me, I felt unworthy, like I wasn't pretty enough or perfect enough to deserve him."

Bettye was silent for a long moment; then her voice surged with conviction. "But that's not true, Andy. It's not my fault. I don't have to focus all my efforts and energy on making somebody else happy at my own expense. God doesn't ask me to please Ricky by forgetting who I am. I have something to offer the world too."

"You've got it, Bettye. Crushing the person you are inside isn't the way to make Ricky, or any man, happy. You cheat him and yourself."

"Yes, I see that now. How could Ricky be happy with me when there was nothing there but a reflection of him? And if I'm just a reflection of him, who am I asking him to love? Oh, Andy, I don't really know who I am. I don't even know what excites or motivates me."

"You love kids. Remember, we talked about it that morning on the cliffs?"

"Yes, but it's too late to have children of my own."

"You talked about working with kids. Volunteer work. Hundreds of kids need someone to love them.

113

Don't waste all that love you have to give, Bettye. Let's pray and ask God to give you the desires of your heart and help you become the person He made you to be. Do you sense it? God's going to open up a whole new world of opportunities for you to explore!"

CHAPTER 11

As Andy bundled up and stepped out into the chill night air, Bettye called after her, "Be careful! There are still patches of ice. It's slippery!"

"I'll be fine. You take care!" Andy walked gingerly over the glazed sidewalk toward the parking lot, the wind slapping her scarf against her face. The air was damp and heavy, ready to burst with unshed rain. After the cozy warmth of the townhouse, the coldness felt both biting and invigorating.

Andy shivered. The wind was rising swiftly, whispering through trees, rustling limbs, and whipping whirlwinds of dead leaves around glowing streetlights.

The whole world is shifting, Andy marveled. *The trees are rocking and the wind is stirring things up. Nothing is standing still. I love that feeling. We're changing. Bettye and I are helping each other change and grow. The wind is blowing the cobwebs out of our minds.*

Just the memory of Bettye's expression as they said good-bye exhilarated her. Bettye had looked so young and rejuvenated; her color was back and her eyes were bright with hope. God was pouring out His blessings. Andy couldn't wait to tell Steve all that God was doing.

She had her chance on Friday evening when Steve drove her to the Cracker Barrel restaurant, one of their favorite places for a casual dinner. As usual the restaurant was noisy and crowded, with people chattering, dishes clattering, and country music rollicking through the speakers.

The hostess led them to a row of small tables, all of them occupied except the center one. As they sat down, Andy wished they had been given a table with some privacy, but it was too late; they were already seated.

After a waitress brought water and took their order, Steve sat back, removed his glasses, and rubbed the bridge of his nose. His casual yellow shirt, open over a gray T-shirt, accentuated his broad shoulders and trim waistline. A strand of russet-brown hair curled over his forehead, giving a hint of the vulnerable boy behind his solemn demeanor.

For a few minutes they engaged in casual chitchat— the weather, work, their plans for the weekend. Steve told her as usual about the latest exploits of his cherished pets —his dog, Danny, and his cat, Tommy. Danny the Dog— a black and white stray Steve had "inherited" from Melissa Manchester while he was producing her album—was something of a legend in Nashville. Steve often took Danny with him to the studios, where the plucky canine had developed an "ear" for music. He would howl at certain songs which later became hits. As Danny's fame spread across Music Row, he began appearing on album covers and in videos, newspaper articles, and supermarket tabloids ("Amazing Psychic Dog Able to Pick Hit

SHELTON & LANDIS

Records"). Danny had even appeared in a special television feature with the newly signed Ricky Van Shelton and proceeded to pick, by howling, Ricky's first top ten record, "Crime of Passion." Steve thought of Danny almost like a son. He felt the same way about Tommy the Cat.

"I was up at three this morning with Tommy," Steve was saying with an amused chuckle. "You know how he won't use a litter box. Well, whenever he wants to go outside, he struts over to a window and starts smacking the blinds. He knows the racket will have me on my feet in a hurry."

"With so little sleep you must be tired tonight," said Andy.

"I am, but I'll survive. How about you? Every time I call, you're out. I haven't seen much of you lately."

"I know. I'm sorry, Steve. I've really been busy."

"So I've noticed. You've been spending a lot of time with Bettye these days." His companionable tone had faded; now there was an edge to his voice. "How's she doing?"

"Great. We've had some awesome prayer times together. The way she lives her faith amazes me. She's stronger than she's ever been."

For a long minute Steve didn't reply. Andy felt the atmosphere between them changing; the lightness in Steve's demeanor had shifted to gloom. He absently tapped the spoon from his place setting against his water glass. A frown furrowed his brow. "So what's going on with Bettye and Ricky?"

Andy formed her answer carefully. "I really don't know. We don't talk about Ricky."

Steve's spoon pinged louder against the glass. He cast

her an accusing glance. "Oh, come on, Andy. Of course you talk about Ricky."

"No, we really don't, Steve."

He sat forward, his blue eyes flashing with unexpected intensity. "Well, let me tell you, things are worse since you started helping Bettye. Ricky's irritable and unmanageable. He's almost impossible to work with. Look how he fired Michael Campbell. I suppose you hear all about this, now that you're renting a room from Michael."

"Michael and I don't really talk about it."

"All right, but Ricky's drinking in the studio now, something he never did before. And he's not hiding his partying from the guys in the band. In fact, all he wants to sing are party songs, drinking songs. Rumors of his affairs are all over Music Row. Columbia has even put the release of his gospel album on hold. Listen, I love the guy, Andy, but I don't think you're helping him at all."

She leaned forward, her elbows on the table. "I'm not trying to help Ricky. I'm trying to help Bettye."

Steve's voice rose with indignation. "I don't think helping Bettye is helping Ricky. You can't rush in and solve everybody's problems. It doesn't work that way, Andy."

"Are you blaming me for Ricky's troubles?"

"No, of course not. I just . . ."

Their conversation broke off as the waitress came with their dinner salads. "Ground pepper?" she asked. She looked at Andy. "Can I get you anything?"

"No, I'm fine." *You can't get me anything; just get me out of here!* Andy poked idly at her salad; her appetite was gone; her stomach was in knots. With bitter irony she recognized one of Ricky's songs playing over the speakers.

I've cried my last tear for you,
wasted my last year on you . . .

Over the guitar beat and Ricky's lyrical tenor, she said, "I care about their marriage, Steve. I care about it more than—"

His fork clattered on the tabletop. "More than us?"

"No, Steve." She felt herself retreating, pulling back like a scolded child. *Why can't I make you understand? You're my future. I love you more than anyone!*

"Okay, I know that wasn't a fair question. Forget I said it." Steve rubbed his forehead slowly, methodically, as if his sinuses were acting up.

I'm giving him a headache, Andy thought dismally. *I'm making him feel awful. I've really messed this up, and it will never get better!*

Steve met Andy's gaze with a disarming directness. "I'm not trying to tell you what to do. I wouldn't do that. But you know what I'm up against. Columbia has invested millions of dollars in Ricky. A lot of people are depending on him. And I feel responsible. I signed him; I brought him into the company.

"But it's not just the business, Andy. You know me well enough to know that. I feel like I'm losing a friend. Ricky used to telephone all the time. Early in the morning, seven-fifteen, he'd call and say, 'Hey, Buck, what's up? Look, I was just reading this magazine and there was a great car in there. You gotta see it.' Or he'd call late at night, from the road, from the bus." Steve's jaw tightened. "Andy, he's stopped calling. He won't even talk to me anymore."

Tears welled in her eyes. "What do you want me to do?"

Before he could reply, the waitress brought their entrees—chicken and dumplings with three vegetables. She looked at their uneaten salads and asked, "Are you finished?"

"Yes, I'm through," said Steve.

"Me, too," said Andy.

The waitress retrieved the salad bowls and beamed her brightest smile. "Okay, now. You two enjoy your meal."

But enjoyment wasn't part of their evening. They ate in silence, picking sullenly at their food, the only sound between them the clattering of Steve's utensils against his plate. Finally he looked up and said, "Andy, I'm not very hungry tonight. How about you? Are you ready to go?"

She nodded and dabbed her lips with the napkin.

Steve drove Andy back to his house in his sporty, two-door BMW. There, she would pick up the red Bronco truck he often lent her. Neither spoke for the first mile or two.

At last he broke the silence. "Well, are you going to talk to me?"

Quietly she said, "I don't feel like you'll hear me."

A long pause, then: "You don't know how I feel."

"No, I don't know how you feel. But you don't know how I feel either."

"Well, good. Then let's just leave it at that."

Andy glanced over at him from the corner of her eye. Steve was sitting ramrod straight, his chin high, his hands gripping the wheel. Lights and shadows played across his chiseled profile, accenting the handsome symmetry of his face. If they weren't arguing, Andy would edge closer to him and nuzzle his cheek. But right now they were worlds apart and might never touch again.

"I don't want to leave it at that," she countered. "This is really important to me, Steve. Bettye is hurting. She's alone. She needs somebody. I've got to be there for her."

Steve pulled the BMW into his driveway, braked, and turned off the ignition. Then he turned in his seat and looked at her, his gaze riveting. "What about me, Andy? What about *me*?"

Her eyes brimmed with tears. "I'm here for you too, Steve."

"Are you? My career is at risk too, you know. Not just Ricky's. Mine. People are questioning me, asking, 'What's going on with Ricky Van?' He doesn't return their calls any more than he returns mine." Steve looked away, speaking more to himself now than to her. "Like I said, Andy, it all comes back to me, because I signed him and I'm the one responsible. It all comes back to me."

"I know, Steve. I know."

He hit the steering wheel with the palm of his hand and said under his breath, "I owe it to the label to guide Ricky as best as I can, and he won't even talk to me!"

Tears ran down Andy's cheeks. "I'm sorry," she murmured.

He looked back at her. There was something in his eyes she hadn't seen before. Was it fear? Pain? "Andy, if you know something that can help, why aren't you helping me?"

"I don't know anything, Steve. I don't!"

He inhaled sharply. He sounded almost subdued

now. "Okay. Maybe not. But I feel like . . . I feel you put other people before me, Andy."

She recoiled. "Steve, you don't really believe that."

Without a word he climbed out of the car and slammed the door. Andy sat unmoving for a long minute, not sure what to do next. Then she pushed open the door, jumped out of the vehicle, and ran up the icy driveway to the porch. Steve was just unlocking the door. Her mouth and throat felt dry as sandpaper. The wind caught her hair and sent it cascading around her face and shoulders in disarray. She clasped his arm and whispered urgently, "Good-bye, Steve. I love you."

He shook his head. "No, Andy. Right now I really don't feel like you love me."

She remained on the porch, the wind catching her tears, as he stepped inside and shut the door. Then she pivoted and walked across the driveway to the red Bronco. She felt guilty taking his truck now. It was ironic that, since her move to Nashville, he let her freely use his vehicles, when sometimes he himself seemed so far beyond her reach.

As she drove home the sky looked especially dark, as if the gloom that had settled over her spirits were blotting out moonlight and starlight and lamplight as well. The dusky road ahead blurred with the surreal distortion of her tears. "Steve's right," she said aloud, accusingly. "I've failed him. He'll never want to marry me, because I haven't focused on him; I haven't helped him; I haven't put his needs first.

"Oh, Lord, maybe I did stick my nose in the wrong place. Here I am trying to help Bettye and Ricky, and I'll probably never have a husband and home of my own!"

She pulled into her driveway and was relieved to see that the house was dark. Good. Michael would be asleep. She could just slip inside and steal quietly to her room.

As she got out of the truck and walked toward the house, she noticed that the wind had changed. It was gusting, moving this way and that, wayward and whimsical as a naughty child, as unpredictable as her own inscrutable future. Not at all like the winds of promise at Bettye's townhouse, which had rejuvenated her spirits. Tonight's wind carried a dark foreboding; it whispered misgivings and buffeted her with doubts.

Maybe I was naive, she conceded with an involuntary shudder. *Maybe this is bigger than all of us.*

C H A P T E R 12

*A*t the end of January, Ricky telephoned Bettye and said, "Can you do me a favor? My mama and daddy's fiftieth anniversary is coming up on February 8th. I can't make it. I'll be on the road. I was hoping you could go and stand in for me. Will you go?"

Without thinking twice, Bettye said, "Of course I'll go, Ricky. Your family is still my family."

"Good, Bettye. Mama and Daddy will be happy to see you. You give them my love and tell them I wish I could be there too, okay?"

"I will, Ricky." She hesitated, then asked, "Are you okay?"

"Sure, Bettye. How about you?"

"I'm doing all right."

"I'm glad to hear it. And, Bettye—you're doing a real swell job keeping up things at the house."

"I told you I would. Ricky, I just wanted to say—"

"Yeah, Bettye?"

"Lately I've been hearing your new song all over the radio. 'Rockin' Years,' your duet with Dolly Parton. It's the most beautiful love song I ever heard."

<u>*124*</u>

"Thanks, Bettye. Dolly's brother wrote the song to honor their parents, but I was thinking of my mama and daddy when I sang it, thinking of their fifty years together."

"I know, Ricky, I know." But what she wanted to say was, *I just wish the couple in the song could be us, Ricky. That's the kind of love and devotion every wife dreams of— the earliest love to the oldest love. It's all I want. I hear you making all those wonderful promises, but it breaks my heart because you're not making them to me.*

On February 7th, the day before Jenks and Eloise's anniversary, Bettye made the eight-hour drive alone to Grit. Over and over she heard "Rockin' Years" playing on the local stations.

> *I'll do everything I can*
> *to make you proud to be my man,*
> *and I'll fulfill all your fantasies.*
> *I guess we're promising a lot,*
> *but for now it's all we got,*
> *and I'll stand by you*
> *through our rockin' years.*
> *Rockin' chairs, rockin' babies,*
> *rock-a-bye, rock of ages,*
> *side by side we'll be together always.*
> *And if you hold me tight when you love me,*
> *that's all I'll ask of you,*
> *and I'll stand by you*
> *through our rockin' years.*
> *I'll be your friend, I'll be your lover,*
> *until the end there'll be no other,*
> *and my heart has only room for one.*

<u>125</u>

Yes, I'll always love you,
and I'll always be here for you,
and I'll stand by you
through our rockin' years.

Bettye found it tragically ironic that Ricky sang so passionately and persuasively of the permanence of love when he was so blatantly disregarding his own marriage. Even when the song wasn't playing, the words echoed in her mind, taunting her with the realization that she and Ricky may never see their golden wedding anniversary. Her heart ached every time she heard her husband's warm, tender voice singing the words that should have been meant for her alone.

That evening, as Bettye entered Grit, she passed the sprawling billboard that proclaimed, "WELCOME TO GRIT, VA. HOME OF RICKY VAN SHELTON." She winced. *Ricky should be coming home with me. This is his home, his family, his town. He should be here celebrating with us.*

She drove on with growing misgivings to the familiar white, two-story frame house. She wondered, *How long can Ricky and I keep up this pretense for our families? Surely one of these days, someone will suspect that our marriage is in trouble. Be careful, Bettye. Don't slip up. One wrong word and everyone will know the truth.*

Judy Underwood, Ricky's older sister, greeted Bettye at the door with a warm embrace. She and Judy had been close friends since childhood, even before Bettye started going with Ricky. "You tell my baby brother we all missed him," said Judy, "but we're sure glad you could be here, Bettye. We couldn't imagine celebrating without you."

Ricky's older brother, Ronnie, gave her a big bear hug too. He had Ricky's sculpted features, but Ronnie wore glasses and sported a solid gray beard. He had his daddy Jenks's quick smile and mischievous twinkle in his eyes. "That little brother of mine better be treating you right," he said with a grin.

Bettye managed a smile. "Sure, Ronnie. You know Ricky."

Jenks and Eloise were ready with embraces too. Eloise told her, "I'm so glad you could come, Bettye. It's going to be a real nice party. We got the church fellowship hall reserved—"

"I reckon 'bout everybody in town will be there," said Jenks with a chuckle. "You tell my boy he missed a right fine party."

"Well, you know he'd be here if he could. He was thinking about you both when he sang 'Rockin' Years.' Have you heard it?"

"We've seen the video," said Jenks. "It's playing everywhere. If you ask me, it's gonna be a number one hit."

"I think so too," said Bettye wistfully.

That evening the family sat around the comfortable little living room reminiscing, laughing, and swapping favorite memories and jokes. "Remember all the jokes Ricky used to play on everybody?" said Judy. "He was always up to some mischief."

"I recall the night he put salt in our bed sheets," said Eloise. "It felt like we'd been to the beach."

"How 'bout the time he put peanut butter in my shoes?" said Jenks. "I reckon I still got peanut butter between my toes. Good thing they wasn't my Sunday shoes."

"Daddy, I remember when you bought him his first guitar," said Judy. "I can still see him on Christmas morning, his eyes lighting up like you'd handed him a million dollars."

"All right, you can laugh, but that guitar was the best J. C. Penney had to offer. And look what that guitar led to."

"Okay, you got him started on the guitar," said Ronnie, "but I got him started on country music."

"With a bribe," said Judy.

"Why not? I told him if he gave up rock and roll and took up country music he could drive my '64 Ford Fairlane. I think he got the best bargain—him on the radio and TV now, singing up a storm. He got what he always wanted, didn't he, Bettye?"

She looked up, startled. "What, Ronnie?" Her mind had wandered as she sat listening to Ricky's childhood exploits. She couldn't help wondering what had happened to the Ricky his family knew and loved.

"I said, Ricky got what he wanted, didn't he?" Ronnie repeated.

She paused, mulling over Ronnie's words. "Yes. I guess you could say Ricky got what he wanted." But silently she wondered, *Does anybody in the world know what Ricky wants these days?*

Throughout her weekend in Grit—especially at the

Bettye at
a year old

Drawing of five-year-old Bettye by
Ricky

Six-year-old Bettye at the Tom
Thumb Wedding at Altavista
Elementary School

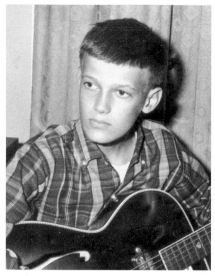

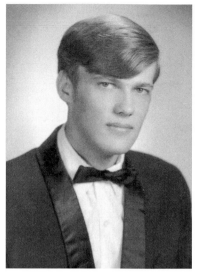

Ricky at age 13

Ricky's high school graduation picture, 1970

Bettye and Ricky in Virginia in 1980

Bettye and Ricky on their wedding day, August 4, 1986, with Jerry Thompson, who married them.

Betty and Ricky with Linda and Jerry Thompson in 1987 at Ricky's first number-one hit-record party given by CBS Records

Ricky with his parents, Eloise and Jenks Shelton, at his induction into the Grand Ole Opry, 1987

Bettye's parents, Earl and Dorothy Witt

Bettye and Ricky at the 1989 Music City News Award Show

Bettye and Ricky
with Roy Rogers,
1990

Bettye and Ricky's home

Four-year-old Andy, right, with her sisters,
Diana, 8, and Anita, 1

Andy at age 18

(left) The Landis girls in 1983: Diana, Andy, Anita, and Jennifer (l to r)

(below) Andy at a recording session with Steve, Paul Franklin, seated, and Sonny Landreth, 1993

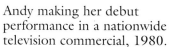

Andy making her debut performance in a nationwide television commercial, 1980.

Andy with Steve after one of her performances in Dallas, 1993

Andy performing in South
Bend, Indiana, 1994

Andy at a photo shoot for her album
cover, 1993

Ricky and Steve
celebrating the
success of
"Loving Proof"
at Columbia
Records, 1988

Bettye and Andy in
Bettye and Ricky's
log home

Bettye and Andy at Bettye and Ricky's beefalo ranch, 1995

Sunday morning service of St. John's Pentecostal Holiness Church and at the golden anniversary party on Sunday afternoon—Bettye couldn't get Ricky and his "Rockin' Years" ballad out of her thoughts. Sitting in the pew beside Eloise and Jenks, she thought about Ricky growing up in this church and sitting in these same pews. As a teenager he had walked this very aisle to the altar to give his heart to Jesus.

Oh, dear Lord, Ricky was saved right here in this sanctuary. It's important that I pray for him here where he first found You. Please make him remember his salvation. Let him remember the commitment he made to You and the commitment he made to me.

She thought, too, about their families. She and Ricky had come from a long line of good marriages. Ricky's folks had just celebrated their golden wedding anniversary; her parents would be celebrating theirs next year.

There's a reason God brought me back here to this church with Ricky's mom and dad, she realized. But what exactly was God trying to tell her? *Lord, are You showing me a promise—that Ricky and I can make it to fifty years too? I don't see how it could be, but if You say it's so, I believe it can happen for Ricky and me!*

CHAPTER 13

When Andy dropped by the townhouse shortly after Bettye's return from Virginia, Linda Thompson, who
had joined them for several prayer sessions, was there
bringing news of her daughter stationed in Iraq. "I just
got a letter and she's doing all right. She thinks the war is
winding down and could end in a matter of weeks. But it
won't be any too soon for me!"

"Tell her the three of us are meeting here in the sanctuary and that we care about her and everyone in that
war," said Andy.

"Tell her we're praying for her, too," said Bettye.

"I will," said Linda.

"Listen," said Bettye, "you two talk while I go toss a
salad. The pizza should be here any time." She held up a
small red tin. "And look what I've got just for you,
Andy."

"Cracked red pepper! Oh, Bettye, you remembered!"

"About time, isn't it? You ask for it every time we
have pizza."

"But to go out and buy it just for me, that's real
friendship!"

"With the steady diet of pizza I feed you, cracked red pepper's the least I can do."

"I love pizza," said Andy. "Don't you, Linda? See? We both love pizza!"

Bettye flashed a bemused smile. "If you say so. Now I'll go see what I can toss into the salad."

"Anything but the kitchen sink," said Andy, sitting down comfortably on the sofa.

"Can't hear you!" Bettye called from the kitchen.

"Just as well. I'm babbling," Andy trilled in a sing-song voice. She glanced at Linda, but Linda wasn't smiling. "What's wrong?" she asked softly.

Linda sat down beside her and whispered, "I'm worried about Bettye."

"So am I," said Andy. "She's had a rough time lately."

"But I'm afraid it's only going to get worse."

"Why? Do you know something I don't know?"

Linda nodded. "I know something Bettye doesn't know."

"Something about Ricky?"

"Plenty about Ricky."

"You mean the rumors?"

"You've heard them too?"

"Yes, from Steve. As Ricky's producer, he hears all kinds of things. He told me there might be other women. But it's only idle speculation, isn't it?"

Linda cast a furtive glance toward the kitchen, then met Andy's gaze squarely. "No, Andy, it's more than that. Jerry told me it's true. And you know my husband. He knows everything that goes on in Nashville. He says the rumors are flying. There are too many not to be true."

"I've asked Bettye about them, and she won't even consider the possibility that Ricky's cheating."

"I know. I've asked her too. She refuses to see it."

"What should we do?"

"I think it's time we both confronted her. She's got to know the truth, Andy, no matter how much it hurts."

"And it will. She believes that man can do no wrong."

"What man?" Bettye came through the kitchen doorway carrying a leafy salad. She set it on the small dining room table. "Tell me. Am I missing some juicy gossip?"

Andy and Linda looked knowingly at each other. "This probably isn't the time to get into this," Andy began. "But then again, there's no good time—"

"It's about what I told you in December when we went on the river boat cruise," said Linda. "The rumors about Ricky."

Bettye rolled her eyes. "You're not going to start that again, are you? Linda? Andy? We've been through this. I told you, Ricky would never do that. I know Ricky. He's a good man."

"You trust Jerry, don't you?" Linda asked gently. "He says the rumors are true, Bettye. People in the industry are talking about Ricky getting drunk after the shows and chasing anything in skirts. They say his whole band is disgusted with his behavior. I'm sorry, Bettye, but we're convinced that Ricky is having affairs."

Bettye flinched as if she'd been punched; she wavered a little but remained standing, her features frozen in disbelief. After a moment she took a deep breath and tears welled in her eyes. "It can't be true," she breathed. "It can't be true." Then her eyes met theirs and she whispered, "But somehow I know it is."

"Maybe it's time you confronted him," said Andy.

"What will I say?"

Andy could feel Bettye's pain piercing her own heart. *Oh, Lord, I feel like we took a knife and stabbed her. Is this going to be too much?*

Bettye caught her breath again and said, "We have to pray for Ricky to come back to the Lord."

"Let's pray now," said Andy.

Bettye sank down in the chair as if her energies were spent. Andy noticed that the youthful innocence in her eyes was gone; she looked like a woman ready to face the truth.

They prayed all evening. The air felt heavy, as oppressive as the burden on their hearts. Andy seldom felt at a loss for words, but tonight she realized there was nothing she could say. She had no words of comfort to ease Bettye's pain. She and Linda had to let Bettye hurt.

Hours later, as Andy said good night, she urged Bettye, "Let Ricky go. Take your hands off him completely and concentrate on *your* relationship with God. Let God take care of Ricky."

"I will. I promise."

Andy gave her a hug. "Will you be okay?"

"Yes," she said, her eyes glistening, "because I understand now why Ricky stopped looking at me. Don't you see, Andy? It all makes sense. He must have felt so guilty, he couldn't look me in the eye. That means the Ricky I love is still there. There's a reason to hope."

<u>*133*</u>

"Oh, Bettye, it amazes me that you can still see the good in him!"

"I've got to, Andy. But I'm going to face him, like you said. He'll be home this week. I'm driving out to the farm and I'm getting the truth, whatever it takes."

As Andy headed home from the sanctuary, she marveled over Bettye's courage and loyalty. *Ricky doesn't know what he has. He's so lost, he can't see it, but I do.* Aloud she said, "Ricky, if you let Bettye go, you're a fool. It'll be the worst thing you've ever done. Somebody else will grab her up so fast your head will spin."

On Sunday morning, as Andy and Steve had breakfast together in his cozy kitchen, the phone rang. Steve answered and handed the receiver to Andy. "It's Bettye. She wants to talk to you."

After Andy said hello, Bettye's voice came back, sounding strained and unnatural. "Andy, I need to talk to you and Buck. Can I come over?"

"Sure, Bettye. We are going to church this morning. Why don't we all go together?"

"All right, Andy. I'm at the farm. I'll be there in an hour."

Andy hung up the phone and looked at Steve. "Something's wrong. Terribly wrong. I could hear it in her voice."

Steve didn't reply. He picked up his newspaper and opened it so that the pages made a rustling sound. An uneasy tension had remained between them since their evening at the Cracker Barrel restaurant. Even now Andy wondered how long their fragile truce could last.

For the next hour she and Steve sat at the round oak table sipping their coffee in contemplative silence, waiting. Steve read the newspaper and absently scratched the ears of his dog, Danny, sitting beside his chair. Andy turned her coffee mug between her palms and gazed around at the comfortable kitchen, bright and gleaming with its twelve-foot-high ceiling, beige tiled floor, oak cabinets, and almond-colored appliances. The morning sun streaming in through the windows along the east wall gave the room a burnished glow.

Andy watched Tommy, Steve's proud black-and-white cat pad silently across the kitchen to the den and jump up on the love seat. The den was filled with forties wood deco furniture; beside the love seat stood two matching chairs with warm green tuck and roll, a floor-model radio, and a lamp with a fringe shade. Andy loved the warmth, peace, and permanence of this small, turn-of-the-century Victorian house. Even when she and Steve were at odds, this house seemed a refuge of tranquillity.

But today the peace will be broken and this room will be filled with pain, Andy thought as she swallowed her coffee. *Bettye is hurting and I don't know if Steve and I can help her.*

Bettye arrived just as Andy was putting on another pot of coffee. "Would you like coffee or juice?" Andy asked as Bettye sat down at the table across from Steve.

"Nothing for me," she said with a little wave of her hand. She looked small and fragile and deeply wounded, Andy noted, the same way she had looked after Ricky told her he didn't love her.

Andy brought her a glass of juice anyway and sat down beside her. She and Steve sipped their coffee and waited for Bettye to speak.

"He told me, Andy," she said at last, her voice breaking. "He told me the truth. He said he's been with other women."

Andy set down her coffee mug. "Oh, Bettye!"

"He said it only happened twice. Both times he was drunk and woke up with a woman he didn't know."

"Ricky told you that himself?" Steve asked.

"Yes, Buck, he told me so himself."

Steve pushed aside his newspaper and stood up. "I can't believe Ricky would ever be involved with somebody else," he said unevenly. "I heard the rumors, and I know Ricky's had his problems, but it's so unlike Ricky."

"That's how I felt too," said Bettye. "Ricky's not himself."

Steve paced back and forth between the table and the counter. "I know Ricky. He was always such a simple, honest, forthright person. A gentleman."

"I'm so worried," said Bettye, "for him and for me. He's so blind to the dangers of what he's doing. And I'm scared for myself. I've slept with him since he's been with these women." She drew in a quiet breath and released it slowly. "And he's still drinking, more than ever. He says it only happened when he got drunk, but he won't—*can't* —give up the beer."

"Do you think he would listen to Steve?" asked Andy.

"He won't talk to anyone. I told him he needs professional help. And spiritual help. He just kept saying, 'I've got to work this out myself. I don't know what I want or what I'm going to do.' Oh, Andy, he didn't say the infidelities wouldn't happen again!"

Steve put his arm around Bettye in an attempt to comfort her. "I'm so sorry," he whispered.

Andy clasped Bettye's hand and said urgently, "Let

136

Ricky go. We've prayed over and over again. Now you've just got to give him to God."

Bettye nodded, her pale blue eyes glazed with tears. "I'm trying to let go. I'm really trying. Please keep praying."

"I will, Bettye. I'll pray harder than ever!"

That morning, as Steve drove the three of them to church, Andy stared out the window at the passing scenery. Winter still held its frigid grip on the earth, shading the world in muted tones—drab grays and browns and olive greens. It seemed a long time before spring would come with brightness, color, and warmth.

Andy thought about Bettye and about herself. It was easy for her to tell Bettye to let go of Ricky and trust him to God. That choice seemed so obvious.

But what about me? Andy reflected. *I keep giving Bettye advice I haven't followed myself. I've been holding on to Steve so hard, afraid of losing him, afraid to trust our future to God. Maybe I should take my own advice. Somebody said, "Any fool can learn from his own mistakes, but a wise man learns from somebody else's mistakes." Can I leave Steve with God, and if we get married someday, great; if we don't, that's okay too?*

Lord, help Bettye to trust Ricky to You, and help me to trust Steve to You, no matter what. No matter what.

On February 27, 1991, the Gulf War ended and Kuwait was freed. Bettye woke that morning with what seemed a revelation: *Give Ricky his freedom.* Was God telling her this? Was it her own need to bring an end to the painful deadlock between them? Or was it Andy's words, *Let him go*? Throughout the morning this strange sense of urgency persisted. On her calendar she wrote, THE WAR ENDS. FREEDOM BEGINS.

By noon Bettye could wait no longer. She found Ricky's tour schedule and telephoned him on the road. When he answered, she exclaimed, "Ricky, I want you to know that I set you free today!"

"Uh, what do you mean, Bettye?"

"You're free. You keep telling me you don't know what you want. And I don't know what you want, but I won't make any more claims on you, Ricky. I want you to find some happiness and peace of mind. If you think you need to be with other women, then you've got my blessing. You go out there and find what it is you want. You just find it. I love you, darling, and I want the best for you, and I'm going to be here for you. I couldn't wait to tell you. Do you hear me, Ricky? You're free!"

There was a long minute of silence on the other end of the line.

"Do you know what I'm saying, Ricky? Do you understand?"

At last his voice came over the wires, quiet, almost humble. "Thank you, Bettye."

"I don't want you feeling guilty anymore," she rushed on. "I can't stand that guilty look in your eyes. You go find what you want, and I'll be waiting. You let me know when you find it, okay?"

"Thank you, Bettye." He still sounded incredulous. "I can't tell you how badly I needed to hear you say that."

"You're going to be all right, Ricky. I'll be here if you need someone to talk to. Anything you need, you call me. I'll be here."

He thanked her again and they said good-bye. As she hung up the phone, she felt a taste of euphoria. She had given him his freedom, but she had also gained her own freedom. She wasn't saying she would give him a divorce; no, she was saying, *I'm your wife. Go out and fool around all you want, and when you make up your mind what you want, then come back and tell me.*

That afternoon she telephoned Andy and told her what she had done. There was a pause; then Andy said, "Goodness, Bettye, I don't know if that's what I was thinking when I said let him go."

"But I feel better, Andy. I feel free myself. It must be the right thing to do."

"But you can't always trust your feelings," said Andy.

139

SHE STAYS

"Maybe you're trying to please Ricky just as you tried to please your father and brothers when you were a little girl."

"Do you really think so?"

"I just know that putting someone in God's hands isn't the same as giving him the freedom to trample your self-respect. Bettye, God created you to be loved, respected, and cared for. Don't let anyone make you feel as if you don't deserve respect, not even Ricky."

"I know you're right, Andy, but right now I just feel relief."

That sense of relief lingered until the second week of March, when Bettye received her telephone bills for the bus, business, and mobile phones. Usually she just forwarded the bills to Ricky's business manager to pay, but for some reason she picked up the bills and began glancing through them, looking at the phone numbers. Strange. There were so many calls made at odd hours of the night, some even from Virginia late on Christmas Eve night, after Ricky had left Bettye at her folks' home. These couldn't be business calls; they were personal calls, and Ricky was still making them as recently as last week!

Aloud she said, "He told me he had been with two women he didn't even know, but this is more than two. He was even calling them when we were home for Christmas, that night when he was drunk. And he's still calling them!" She felt a sinking sensation in the pit of her stomach. "Oh, Lord, what in the world was I doing giving this man his freedom? Andy was right. How could I have been so foolish?" Then she realized. *I was listening to my old thoughts!*

With trembling hands she picked up the phone and

dialed Ricky's bus number. When he answered, she said stiffly, "Ricky, this is Bettye."

"Yeah?" He sounded wary.

"Ricky—" Her voice quavered slightly. "Ricky, there are a whole lot of strange numbers on your phone bills for calls you made at all hours of the night to other towns and other states. Is—is there something you have to tell me?"

He was quiet a moment, then his voice came out rough as gravel. "I'll tell you when I come home, Bettye. I'll be coming in on Monday, the 18th. You be there at the farm waiting, okay?" He paused again, then said meaningfully, "I'll tell you *everything* when I get home."

In a small voice she answered, "Okay, Ricky."

On March 18th, Bettye drove out to the farm early in the morning just as the sun was cresting the meadows. In spite of the chill, the air carried the first budding scents of spring. She knew it would be hours before Ricky's bus pulled in, but she wanted time to settle in, straighten things up, and make sure the cupboards were stocked and a pot of coffee was brewing.

She sensed that this day would be pivotal in their relationship. Years from now they might mark the shifting direction of their lives by what was said and done this day. But for all its significance, the hours ticked by at a snail's pace. Bettye waited. She walked back and forth between the kitchen and living room, taking comfort in familiar furnishings and mementos—Ricky's Coca-Cola clock and thermometer on the wall; the antique hutch filled with their favorite memorabilia, china dishes, and crystal; her small cherry wood writing desk beside the mohair chair. She watched out the window for Ricky's bus. She waited some more.

As Bettye's anxiety mounted, she reached for the telephone and dialed. "I've got to talk to Andy." After she had filled Andy in about Ricky's homecoming, she said, "Please pray. I know this will be a day of facing a side of Ricky I've dreaded."

"You're in a spiritual battle," Andy told her. "Get your Bible. I want to read you Ephesians six, verses ten through seventeen, about putting on the armor of God so you can stand against evil."

As Andy read, Bettye caught a vision of a warrior marching to battle, dragging one foot after the other, so exhausted he could barely stand. Wounded and bleeding, he dropped his shield, then pulled off his helmet and dropped it too. Unable to bear the weight of his armor, he loosened it and let it fall to the ground. Finally, with no strength left, he lost grip of his sword. Crawling into battle without weapons or protection, the warrior seemed doomed to defeat.

Then Bettye saw the warrior's armor-bearer following behind, picking up his shield, his helmet, his armor, and sword. Speaking words of encouragement, he placed the warrior's helmet back on his head and gave him his shield and sword, so he wouldn't be defenseless when the battle raged.

Bettye knew immediately that she was the battle-weary warrior and that God had sent Andy to be her armor-bearer. Andy couldn't fight Bettye's battles for her, but she was making sure Bettye was protected and prepared!

When Andy finished reading the Scriptures she prayed for Bettye over the phone; then in a firm, compelling voice she urged, "Stand your ground. Draw a line that you will not cross. Remember your identity in Christ. You know how you should be treated. If Ricky can't accept that, give him the freedom to choose a life without you. If he leaves, remember that God has something better for you."

"I know, Andy. God is with me. He's taken my fear away, and He's given me *His* confidence. I know whatever fiery darts are thrown at me today, Jesus will win the battle."

The waiting was easier now. As Bettye watched out the window she realized she felt strong, unusually calm, protected by His Spirit. Whatever happened with Ricky, God was in charge.

And then, suddenly, she spotted the huge silver bus rolling up the long driveway. It stopped in front of the garage, and after a moment Ricky got out. From the window she watched him walking up the yard to the house with his bags. It wasn't his usual carefree gait; his head was down and he was taking slow, purposeful strides.

She met him at the door wearing a simple spring dress made of soft, clingy cotton. He stood and looked in her eyes for a long time. She couldn't tell what he was thinking. He didn't smile. He said simply, "Let me get settled in and we'll talk."

For the first time she had the impression he was as anxious to get this over with as she was. As he took his luggage upstairs, she sat waiting for him in the living room, her thoughts racing. *Now what? How much more am I going to have to endure? Help me, Lord!*

When he came back downstairs, she noticed he had changed into his old jeans and a sweatshirt, but there was something else different about him. A sense of urgency.

He looked directly at her and seemed eager to talk. He sat down in his recliner by the fireplace and she moved over to the hearth, almost at his knees. He sat forward, his feet flat on the floor and his hands on the cushioned arms of the chair, as if he had determined to keep nothing back.

He said, "Bettye, when you called me the other day, I knew I was going to tell you the truth. And these last two days, one thing kept going through my mind. All I've heard for the last two days is, 'The truth will set you free.' It's from the Bible."

"Yes, I know."

"Well, I remember reading it. I remember. It came back to me. That's all I heard for two days . . . 'the truth will set you free.' And I knew I had to tell you, Bettye. I have to tell you everything."

"I want to know it all, Ricky. When this day is over, I don't want there to be any question in my mind left unanswered."

"There won't be. I'll tell you anything you ask me."

And he did. For two solid, painful, excruciating hours he revealed all he could remember of those drunken, partying episodes—the different women, the different times, the different places.

Bettye reeled under the impact of his words. There were so many affairs, so many betrayals. It was as if he couldn't wait to get it all off his chest.

As hard as it was, Bettye asked every awful, humiliating question a wife would ever want to know. It was as if they were in a courtroom, she the interrogator, he the witness. Her voice was void of emotion, without acrimony or blame.

144

"Were they pretty?"

"Were they young?"

"Were they better built than me?"

"Were they blondes? Brunettes?"

"Were they better in bed?"

She asked the questions, and he replied. And when she didn't ask something that he wanted to admit, he went ahead and told her anyway. She sat facing him on the hearth; her fingers traced the inlaid arrowheads they had found together on the farm. She recalled the happy hours they had spent searching the fields and their joy when they found the "perfect" arrowhead.

When the hearth got too hard, she moved to the floor and sat at Ricky's feet. She urged him to say it all. The truth couldn't be stopped because of emotion. Guilt couldn't stop it; shame, anger, pain, nothing could keep the facts from being revealed.

Bettye reached the point where she couldn't think of any more questions. She felt numb. She gazed around the room at their belongings. Ricky's favorite old guitars and violin hung on the walls; his childhood toys—tractors, trucks, and cars—lined the windowsills. Her eyes swept over the floral, cream-colored sofa where she loved to sit and rub Ricky's feet, and the old trunk that served as a coffee table—the first piece of furniture her dad had built for her mom almost fifty years ago. These cherished possessions offered little comfort now in the stunning glare of truth.

Yes, there was truth in this room for the first time in months, so much truth it almost killed her. Ricky's betrayal went beyond their wedding vows; he had betrayed their home, their past and future, their memories and dreams. The stark reality of his infidelities pierced her, imbedding her mind with visual images too loathsome to imagine. It was sordid and sick, and she felt weak, nauseated, and weary beyond words. But she refused to allow the emotion to set in yet.

After several minutes of silence, Ricky said, "Bettye, I still don't know what I want. I go out and get drunk and wake up with some woman. I don't know what to do about it."

"Ricky, if you would just stop drinking . . ."

"I can't, Bettye. I've tried. God knows I've tried. Do you think I like not having control?"

She moved back up to the hearth and looked deep into his eyes. Strangely, as much as his confession had repulsed and wounded her, she felt closer to him now than she had in months. The wall between them had crumbled. He looked like the Ricky she had fallen in love with; his solemn green eyes were open and vulnerable; there was honesty in the sturdy planes and angles of his face, as if he had stripped away the mask to expose the flawed, needy, human man beneath the veneer.

God is working here, she realized, *even in this hurtful situation. God is dealing with Ricky, I know it. Before, there was such darkness around him, but now he's hearing the Word in his heart—"the truth will set you free." There's a glimmer of light.*

"Ricky," she said with sudden resolve, "I hate everything you've described to me, but I don't hate you. I still see a spark of goodness in you, and I still love you. Still you've got to make a decision. I will not allow this to continue. I draw the line tonight. If you want me to continue to be your wife, I'm going to be the only woman in your life from this point on. I will not share you with anybody else."

"But, Bettye, you said—"

"I was wrong when I gave you your freedom to be with anyone. That was not from God. I was wrong, and I know that now. You have to decide between me and them."

"I don't know, Bettye. I told you I don't know what I want."

"Then we've got to agree right now, until you know, you will not be with another woman, or else you are to divorce me. I will not be your wife and have you be with other women. The choice is yours. You either choose me or you choose the other women. And, Ricky, if you can't make that decision, I'll make it for you."

"Bettye, give me some time."

"I will, but in the time you're trying to find out what you want, you've got to promise me there will be no other women; you will not go to bed with another woman until you decide."

He nodded, fatigue etched in his features. "All right, I will not be with another woman until I decide what I want."

Bettye stood up. Exhaustion was settling into her bones. She was too tired even to drive back to her townhouse. There was no reason to leave anyway. The coldness and alienation that had driven her from this house were gone. She gazed at Ricky and said, "I'm going upstairs to bed."

He stood up too and looked at her as if he had

glimpsed a side of her he hadn't seen before. "Okay, Bettye. I'll be right here." His voice was subdued, polite. "I'm just gonna stretch out here on the couch. You need anything, you just holler."

CHAPTER 15

*T*he same Monday that Bettye heard Ricky's confession, Andy received a phone call from Steve. He sounded on edge, upset; yet he spoke in hushed tones. "Can you come over to the house tonight for dinner, Andy? I have something to ask you."

"Sure, I'll be there," she replied, resisting the urge to ask what he wanted. It didn't sound like he planned to kiss and make up. With their relationship growing increasingly strained, she had even stopped wearing her engagement ring. They were engaged, yet not engaged. They had put their entire future on hold.

That evening, Andy arrived at Steve's house before he did. She was dressed casually in a denim shirt, faded jeans, and black boots. She waited inside, pacing, wondering if it was possible for her relationship with Steve to deteriorate even further. The living room, done in mauve, beige, and brown accents, was cozy and warm. Usually Andy felt so at home in this room, but not tonight.

Steve's dog, Danny, watched her curiously, and Tommy rubbed against her leg and meowed. She scooped the cat up in her arms and nuzzled the top of his furry

149

head with her chin. "I wish you could talk, Tommy," she whispered against his black velvet ear. "I bet you could tell me what's going on."

Finally she heard the door open. Steve burst in, shut the door hard behind him, and stormed across the room toward her, his eyes blazing. His solid six-foot frame looked taller than usual. He stopped directly in front of her and put his hands on his hips, his face ashen. "I want you to tell me the truth, Andy."

Her heart raced with alarm. She put down the cat and stammered, "Uh, I will if I can."

His words exploded like fireworks. "Is Bettye having an affair?"

Andy felt shock waves ripple along her spine. "No! Absolutely not!"

"Are you positive?"

"Of course I'm positive."

"If you know something, you have to tell me," Steve said emphatically.

"I give you my word she's not."

He led her over to the sofa and they sat down. He gazed levelly at her. "Are you telling me the truth, Andy?"

"Yes, Steve, I'm telling the truth. I would know if Bettye were having an affair."

"Are you sure you would know?"

"Yes. She's either at her house cleaning, or she's at the townhouse with me. You know how often we're together. And we call each other all the time. She tells me everything." She searched his eyes. "Steve, where did you get such an idea?"

He sat back and drew in a deep breath. "There are rumors going around—"

"Rumors about Bettye?"

"Yes. Rumors of an affair. I've heard them myself. People have come right out and asked me about it."

"What did you say?"

"I told them it was out of the question. I said I'd know if something like that were going on, because Bettye and my fiancee are close friends. But it made me sick to think this could happen and you might know and not tell me."

"I wouldn't do that to you, Steve. You must know that."

"Right now I don't know what to think."

"Who could be spreading such garbage about Bettye?"

"It's either people who are awfully misinformed or business associates of Ricky's—people who think they're doing him a favor by protecting his interests."

"By destroying Bettye? They're setting her up, Steve. It's not fair. Do you know how she's going to feel when she hears about this?"

Steve sat forward and seized her hand. "No, Andy. You are not to tell her under any circumstances. Do you understand? This is serious. You have to stay out of it."

Andy began to weep. "Steve, I'm sorry. I can't—"

"What do you mean, you can't?"

"I can't keep it from her. I don't know if you'll ever forgive me, but—I have to tell her."

His dark brows arched. "I can't believe you'd even think of telling her—after I've asked you not to."

"She needs to know what people are saying. Her rep-

151

utation is at stake. And maybe her financial future. I think she needs to talk to a lawyer."

Steve removed his glasses and rubbed his temples. The tendons along his jaw tightened. "All right. Tell her if you have to, but if she confronts Ricky, ask her to keep my name out of it. Yours and mine."

"I will. I'll tell her to keep us out of it."

"Are you sure she'll be careful with this information? Do you have any idea how she'll react?"

Andy dabbed the moisture from her eyelids. "I—I give you my word that Bettye will handle this with integrity and grace. I'll be responsible if she doesn't."

Steve threw up his hands in exasperation. "Oh, great! You'll be responsible? Sometimes you drive me crazy, Andy!"

"I know, but it'll be all right, Steve. I promise. Thank you for trusting me."

He didn't reply. Instead, he picked up Tommy and cradled the cat in his arms like a child. Almost to himself he muttered, "If that marriage is saved, it will be a miracle!"

"That's what I'm counting on," said Andy. She leaned over and brushed a kiss on Steve's lips, but he kept his gaze on Tommy. Something within him had turned away and closed her out and she had no way on earth to bring him back.

Early the next morning Andy telephoned Bettye. When she couldn't reach her at the townhouse, she called the farm. She got the answering machine, but as soon as she gave her name, Bettye broke in. "I'm here, Andy."

"So early in the morning?"

"I spent the night. It's a long story. I'll tell you when I see you."

"I was hoping we could get together today. Can I come out to the farm?"

"Now? Can it wait? I was thinking of going—"

"It's important, Bettye. I need to see you now."

"Well, all right, if it's that urgent."

"It is, Bettye. Is Ricky there?"

"No. He's in Nashville at the recording studio all day."

"Good. Then I'll be there in an hour."

For Andy, the long drive out to the farm seemed much bleaker than it had that weekend in November. What had started out last fall as a challenge, a mission of mercy, had turned dark and ugly, mired in a sludge of complications, caveats, and painful consequences. Once again Andy found herself putting Bettye's needs above her fiancé's; once more Steve saw her actions as a betrayal. Perhaps this was God's way of telling her their relationship wasn't meant to be; yet everything inside her told her Steve Buckingham was the man God had chosen for her. Then why did God keep placing her in these untenable situations? And why did she feel as if she were fighting her battles alone?

When she arrived at the farmhouse, Bettye was already standing in the doorway, waiting to greet her. Her expression looked changed somehow; there was a quiet dignity Andy hadn't seen before. They embraced, then went inside and sat down at the breakfast nook that overlooked the Cumberland River. Bettye already had coffee, wheat toast, and fresh fruit on the table.

They chatted for a few minutes about the weather and

the farm. Then Bettye told her quietly, haltingly, about Ricky's confession. When she finished, she sighed and said, "The possibility of divorce has become more real to me, Andy. Not that I want to divorce Ricky. But for the first time I realize he might choose the carefree life of a bachelor with lots of women."

Andy sipped her coffee and felt her courage waning. She couldn't bear the idea of giving Bettye even more bad news. Perhaps she should keep her mouth shut and let Bettye find out about the rumor on her own. But no. Even after hearing Ricky's confession from his own lips, Bettye still looked entirely too innocent and trusting. She needed to know what she was up against.

Bettye poured more coffee. "You're awfully quiet, Andy. Are you okay?"

"Yes, Bettye." Andy realized she was twisting her paper napkin into a ragged snake. "It's just—I don't know how to say this—"

"Say what, Andy? I've never seen you this way before. You seem so nervous. Something really has you shook up."

Andy reached over and patted Bettye's hand. "It's just . . . I've got to tell you something, and you've got to promise that Ricky will never know where it came from. I promised Steve we wouldn't let Ricky know, I promised him. Bettye, promise me he won't find out. You can't involve Steve; I shouldn't be involving him."

"Andy, you're talking in riddles. What does Buck have to do with this?"

"Do you promise?"

"Yes, of course. For heaven's sake, Andy, just tell me!"

Andy chose her words carefully. "I think it's time for you to look out for yourself, Bettye. It's time for you to have all the information so that you can act wisely." Andy closed her eyes and forced out the words. "You need to know, um, there is a rumor going around that you are having an affair."

Bettye stiffened. She set her coffee cup down hard, the liquid sloshing over the rim into the saucer. "No. Nobody would say that."

Andy began to weep. "I'm sorry, but it's true."

Tears glazed Bettye's eyes. "I can't believe it. Who would make up such lies? Who would want to hurt me like that?"

"I don't know. Maybe someone wants to discredit you to make Ricky look good."

"But why?"

"Maybe, if you two divorce, his fans will think you drove him to it. They'll take his side. Or maybe his lawyer could say Ricky heard you were having an affair and went off the deep end. That way, he could keep his money. I don't know."

"No, Andy. Nobody would destroy a person like that. Think what it would do to my parents. And Ricky's parents!"

Andy reached across the table and gripped Bettye's hands. They were both sobbing now. "I'm so sorry, Bettye. You've got to be on guard and not trust everyone around Ricky."

Bettye choked back her tears. "I feel so helpless and small. There's no way to stop it, is there, Andy? People will believe it's true."

<u>155</u>

"No, Bettye. We'll find a way out. God always has the last say."

Bettye dried her eyes and a look of quiet resolve settled on her face. "I've got to talk to Ricky. I have to know if he's aware of this rumor."

Andy cringed. "Please, Bettye," she begged, "whatever you do, keep Steve and me out of it!"

Bettye nodded. "Don't worry. I won't mention you or Buck."

Driving home that evening, Andy fought the impulse to run.

I've done it again, Lord, she lamented. *Jeopardized my fiancé, devastated my friend. Because of me, we'll all end up in the poor house scrubbing floors.*

Her spirits plummeted. She was caught by a whirlwind of circumstance and had no place to flee. Darkness was palpable and shadows deep, and it seemed winter's twisted, barren trees loomed for attack.

"Lord," she whispered into the darkness of her vehicle, "if there was ever a time Bettye and I needed to be surrounded and protected by Your biggest, mightiest angels, this is it!"

CHAPTER 16

When Ricky arrived home from the recording studio that evening, Bettye was waiting for him. She was wearing a white cotton T-shirt tucked into tight blue jeans. She was sitting in his brown high-back La-Z-Boy by the fireplace, watching the flames dance and crackle as they devoured the dry logs. The only other sound was the raw wind rustling the wind chimes that hung over the porch just outside the sliding glass doors. Except for the warm glow of the fire, the house felt chilled. Bettye's palms felt cold; her heart felt encased in ice.

Ricky was humming as he sauntered into the living room. Seeing her, he stopped and offered a quizzical smile. "Hi, Bettye. Well, I'm here. You called and said you had something important to talk about."

She looked up at him without smiling. "Yes, Ricky."

He peeled off his black leather jacket and tossed it over the back of the couch. He was wearing a plaid brown shirt and Levi's. "I figured we said everything we had to say last night. I spilled my guts. What else is there to say?"

He walked past his hand-carved cigar-store Indian to the kitchen and paused by the L-shaped oak counter. His collection of fifties-style cookie jars lined the tops of the high oak cabinets. Bettye could still remember his childlike glee each time he brought a new one home from his travels. "I'm gonna grab me a beer," he said, opening the refrigerator. "You want one?"

"No, Ricky."

He opened a bottle and came back to the couch and sat down. He took a long swallow. "Like I said last night, Bettye, I still don't know what I—"

"This isn't about you, Ricky. It's about me."

He took another swig. "Okay, Bettye. I'm listening."

She ran her hand over the cushioned arm of the chair, her fingernails digging into the nubby material and moving down to the smooth wooden dowel that supported the arm. She forced her voice to remain steady. "I heard something today, Ricky. Something that upset me a whole lot."

His eyes showed a hint of alarm. "Is everybody back home okay?"

"Yes, Ricky. It's nothing like that."

He settled back, relaxing on the comfortable beige sofa, and tipped his bottle up again. "So, okay, Bettye, what's this all about?"

"It's a rumor I heard, Ricky." Her heart started hammering, drowning out the sound of her own voice. She could already picture the outrage that would sweep over Ricky's face when she told him what was being said about her. She had to choose her words carefully. "Ricky, would it surprise you to know that some associates of yours may have worked out a scheme to protect your public image by destroying my good name?"

"What are you talking about, Bettye?"

"Rumors are going around that I'm having an affair."

Ricky took another long swallow of his beer.

"Did you hear me, Ricky? I said—"

"I heard you, Bettye."

"You know it's not true. I've never cheated on you, Ricky."

"I know that, Bettye."

"Then do you think someone's spreading these rumors to protect your image?"

"Probably." His voice remained nonchalant. "I'd expect so. I hire people to look out for me, you know that."

Bettye felt the coldness in her chest spread through her limbs like ice water. "At my expense?"

"That's what I pay them for. They work for me; they're supposed to protect my interests."

Bettye felt the numbing iciness inside her turn to heat. "You mean you would allow people to work for you knowing they're capable of putting out such low, underhanded trash like this? You'd let them destroy your wife's reputation?"

Ricky ran his thumb around the opening of his bottle. "It just shows me they're good at what they do."

Bettye recoiled, as if she'd been socked in the stomach. For a moment she couldn't catch her breath. "Good grief, Ricky, what's happened to you?"

He put his bottle down on the coffee table—the trunk her dad had built so long ago. "Don't worry, Bettye. I'm not going to let them ruin your good name. But I can see where they might've come up with the idea."

Bettye sank back in her chair. She was beginning to see how dark and reprobate Ricky had become. "Ricky, listen to what you're saying," she pleaded. "Listen to

159

yourself. Are you saying you want these people around you even though they'd do things like this?"

Ricky's brow furrowed, as if he couldn't understand what all the fuss was about. "That's the way you have to do things in this world today."

She sat forward, facing him. "The Ricky I know never would have allowed something like this. The Ricky I know is a man of integrity and principles. He's always for the right, for fairness, the justice of things. You're not the Ricky I know."

He reached for his bottle and turned it between his palms. "Come on, Bettye. Don't give me this. Like I said, it's nothing personal. It's just business."

"No, it's not just business!" The heat in her veins was flaming now. The words leapt from her lips. "What you're saying, Ricky, is that you don't have any principles anymore. You're a liar, you're an adulterer, you're a fornicator. You've betrayed your vows to your wife, and you don't care. Is all of this true? This is who you are right now, isn't it!"

He shifted his torso and set his empty bottle on the hardwood floor by his feet. "Bettye, this kinda talk isn't doing either of us any good. I'm gonna go get myself another beer."

"Wait, Ricky. Can I tell you what I see right now in your life?"

He sat back and drummed his fingers on the arm of the couch. His jaw hardened and his lips tightened. His eyelids seemed heavy, shadowing his eyes. He was closing her out.

When he didn't reply, Bettye went on with fresh urgency. "Ricky, I see a battle being fought over you—the battle between good and evil. Right now, the evil's winning out. Everything you're doing is what the evil side wants you to do."

He scowled and turned his gaze to the dying embers in the fireplace and to his painted model cars lining the polished oak mantle. His fingers were still thrumming the couch and his foot was tapping now with a nervous energy, as if he could barely suppress the urge to spring up and flee.

Bettye continued, drilling him with her words. "Ricky, I can just see the devil now, wringing his hands and saying, 'Yeah, he's my boy. I've got him right where I want him!'

"I know there's still a little light of goodness left inside of you, Ricky. It's almost gone; but it's still there; I know it is. It's struggling so hard to live and grow and shine out of that darkness. The devil wants you on his side and in his camp, because thousands of people are watching you; so many young people idolize you. It's up to you whether they idolize you as a drunk, a curser, a partying animal, and a lustful man full of greed, or whether they idolize you as a man of God."

He looked up sharply at her. His fingers stopped drumming and his foot stopped tapping. "God?" he barked. "What's God got to do with what's happening between you and me?"

Bettye's voice broke with emotion. "Don't you see, Ricky? He's got everything to do with us. That's what this whole thing is about. The battle between God and the devil."

Ricky stood up and raked his fingers through his chestnut brown hair. He looked at her with lightning in his navy-green eyes. "Bettye, you've lost your mind! What's wrong with you? God doesn't even know we exist!"

His words stunned her. She collapsed back in her chair, suddenly weak. "How can you say that, Ricky? You used to know God. You knew Him as a teenager."

He paced the floor, his brown boots clicking on the wood. "Do you think with everything going on in this world right now—the war, famine, people dying all over the place—do you think God has time to worry about what's going on between you and me?"

"Where is this coming from, Ricky? Ask yourself—who's telling me these lies that God doesn't know we exist? It's the devil telling you that."

He took long strides back and forth across the sprawling, rectangular room, hitting his knuckles against his palm. "Listen, Bettye, I talked to you; I told you what you wanted to know. I won't let these people ruin your reputation, so don't worry about it. Now is there anything else?"

She lowered her gaze. "No, nothing else."

"All right. Fine. Then I guess we have nothing more to talk about." He strode back to the kitchen and grabbed another beer from the refrigerator.

Wordlessly she gathered her things—a small leather bag and her short-waisted blue denim jacket—and headed for the door. She took one last glance back at her husband. He was settling down in his recliner with his beer and aiming the remote control at the TV screen. With a

162

sinking sensation she realized she had done all she could here. Ricky was out of her hands. It was time now to think about herself. She felt alone, helpless, and vulnerable. It was time to see a lawyer.

*T*he next day a friend gave Bettye the name of a lawyer and she got in for an appointment that very afternoon. But from the moment she entered his office and sat down, she felt a strange sense of foreboding.

"What brings you here today, Mrs. Shelton?" the man asked as he jotted something on the note pad on his wide mahogany desk.

For a long minute she didn't answer. Finally she found her courage and murmured, "I think I may need some legal advice."

"All right. Why don't you tell me all about it?"

She shifted in her chair, adjusting her purse in her lap. "I . . . I'm separated from my husband, not officially, but we're having some problems, and I—"

"Your husband?"

"Yes. He's in the entertainment industry."

"Oh? What does he do?"

"He's a country music singer."

"Really?" The attorney flashed a knowing expression and his eyebrows arched. "Mrs. Shelton, you don't mean—?"

"My husband is Ricky Van Shelton."

The man sat forward and placed his elbows squarely on his desk. His fingertips formed a little pyramid. "I'm sure I can help you, Mrs. Shelton. Tell me the whole story. From the beginning."

In a quiet, pained voice she told him everything. As she spoke she felt a suffocating sensation come over her. She wanted to get up and run, but she couldn't. Why did she feel cornered? The lawyer sat watching her, his eyes never moving from her for an instant. She realized with a jolt that he was grinning—he was actually grinning.

When she had told him all she could think of, she said, "I'm not sure why I'm here, except I feel that I need to protect myself. I need you to help me. Where do I stand legally?"

The man stood up and began pacing the floor, rubbing his hands together with an odd sort of glee. "Honey, you don't have a thing to worry about," he told her, his voice buoyant as helium and smooth as satin. "You just leave everything in my hands. That boy of yours is going to pay everything to you. You can have anything you want."

"But I don't want—" Bettye began, flustered.

"Honey, don't forget," the lawyer said, still grinning, "we're in the Bible belt. You live in a small county. We'll have the divorce in your county, because they're even more conservative than the Nashville courts. We'll file first to make sure it's there. Those old-time farmers out there on the jury won't take to a big, famous man—that you helped make famous—turning his back on you."

Bettye could feel herself being pushed back in her chair by the malevolence in the man's words. "I didn't come in here to talk about a divorce," she countered. "I just don't want to lose everything I've worked hard for. I feel like, if I'm not careful, I could walk away from this and have to start my life all over again with nothing."

The lawyer's excitement was growing. "Don't you worry, honey. We'll have everything that man ever made. You don't have to leave him a red cent. If you want to leave him a pair of socks, we'll make sure they don't match!"

Bettye stood up and gripped the arm of her chair. Her ankles felt weak. What if she fainted right here on the spot? "Thank you," she said warily. "I . . . I'll think about what you said."

The attorney was still all Cheshire grin. "All you've got to do is call me, Mrs. Shelton. We can get it started right now. Your husband has already admitted to adultery. That's all you need, sweetheart, that's all you need. We can take care of the rest of it." With a flourish he handed her his business card. "Just call me. We'll take it from there."

Bettye couldn't get out of his office fast enough.

That evening, still reeling from the events of the past few days, Bettye went to see her friend, Linda Thompson. She desperately needed to see someone who could give her a motherly hug and some good advice. Linda came through with both the hug and the advice. "You go see my attorney," she told Bettye. "Trust me. He's a man of faith and integrity. You need to talk to this man."

Bettye had had her fill of lawyers, but what choice did she have?

The next day she made an appointment for later that afternoon. Once again she found herself entering a strange office and facing an attorney she didn't know. But this time she sensed a difference in the atmosphere—light instead of darkness, hope instead of oppression. The man —years older than she and possessing a fatherly comportment—stood up and shook her hand with genuine warmth and concern. She felt pleasantly reassured.

As she had done before, she told him who she was and who Ricky was, and related the series of events that had brought her to his office. He listened patiently and when she had finished, he asked, to her surprise, "What type of church life has Ricky had?"

She sat in silence for a moment, processing his question. Incredibly, this man was interested in Ricky's *spiritual* condition! She told him about Ricky's Christian heritage and her own, concluding with, "So you see, our parents are Christians; we were raised in the church and saved as teenagers; but as adults we broke away from our faith—until last November, when I gave my life back to God."

The attorney nodded several times, carefully taking in all that she said. When she had finished, he sat forward and looked at her with wise, penetrating eyes. "Now, Mrs. Shelton, I need to know, what is it you want?"

From the depths of her heart she said, "I want my marriage restored."

He sat back and folded his hands on the desk. "All right, I'll give you advice. First, I'll tell you what you need to do to protect your financial security, and then I'm going to tell you what I think you need to do to restore your marriage."

She had no idea what he meant, but she nodded anyway.

"Right now," he went on in his well modulated voice, "if you chose to, you could probably get most of what your husband has—if you *chose* to. He has admitted to adultery and that is grounds for divorce. You were the one who brought him to Nashville, then worked and supported him while he established his music career. You even introduced him to the people who launched his career. To a large degree, you are responsible for his success. The courts would probably see that you got whatever you asked from this man, so that you would be financially secure for the rest of your life.

"Here's what you would have to do if you chose to go that route. Never allow yourself to be alone with your husband in your house again. You see, we would need to prove to a court that you have not had sex with him since you found out that he committed adultery. Because if you slept with him after knowing of his adultery, it would mean you forgave him, and that could no longer be used as grounds for divorce.

"What I suggest is that you bring somebody into the house to live with the two of you, someone who could testify that you were sleeping in separate beds."

"But, as I told you," said Bettye, "I'm not living at the farmhouse anymore; I'm living in my townhouse in Nashville."

"Then you need to give up your townhouse and move back immediately into your own home."

"But why? Ricky wanted me to leave."

"Maybe so, but if you remain in the townhouse, your husband could actually file for a divorce on grounds of desertion. His lawyers could claim that he didn't leave you; you left him."

Bettye put her head back and closed her eyes. Tears glistened on her lids but she forced them back. How much more twisted and convoluted would things get before she saw a glimmer of light?

The fatherly attorney sat back in his chair and smiled. His eyes crinkled with compassion as he said, "Mrs. Shelton, I've given you legal advice. Now I'll give you some advice that would ruin all your chances of ever winning out financially in a divorce settlement."

She looked at him, perplexed. "I don't understand."

He leaned forward across the desk and said with a warm, conspiratorial air, "Be a wife to your husband. Prove to him that you're still strong and dedicated enough to love him and keep him. That's what I advise you to do."

His voice took on a cautionary note. "But if you do that, you'll lose all opportunities of winning in a divorce suit. But if you *don't* do that, you'll not have an opportunity to win him back as your husband." He paused and cleared his throat, giving her a moment for his words to sink in. "So think about it carefully, Mrs. Shelton. If your husband comes to you at any time and wants to reach out to you, you need to decide right then and there, 'Will I be a wife to him or will I secure my future?' "

As the significance of his words took hold Bettye's hopes rose. Here was a man highly esteemed in his profession, and he was telling her she needed to be a wife to her husband! She wanted to reach across the desk and hug this benevolent man.

She stood up, clasped his hand, and declared, "You don't know how grateful I am to have met you!"

Driving back to her townhouse, Bettye felt more

hopeful than she had in weeks. But her elation diminished as she thought about the choices facing her. If she stayed in the townhouse, Ricky could sue her for desertion; if she returned to the farm to be a wife to her husband, she would be risking her financial future.

Hard choices? Not really, because Bettye knew exactly what she wanted.

CHAPTER 18

*T*hat evening, after returning from her visit with the lawyer, Bettye realized her thoughts had crystallized into a clearer vision of her marriage than she'd had in a long time. She sat down at her desk in the townhouse and began writing a letter to Ricky. It was time to tell him, in writing, how she felt about their marriage and to underscore the fact that he had to make a choice—soon!

Ricky, I've been thinking a lot about the fact that the "spark of desire" has left our relationship. I remember the feelings of excitement, discovery, desire, and newness in the beginning of every relationship I've ever had. New flings always start out with a honeymoon.

I believe adults need to decide what kind of relationship they want for the rest of their lives—a relationship that will be there when the honeymoon is over. Maybe that's what God intended when he allowed the "sexual spark" to disappear.

Maybe desire is supposed to be replaced with better, higher feelings. Mature love comes when two people can enrich one another, support each other's dreams, accept each other's faults, dignify one another to the world, and love the qualities that they value in each other—qualities like honesty, compassion, understanding, integrity, patience, and loyalty. Two people should work hard side by side to bring happiness and peace into their hearts, so that when they lie together, not only are they able to satisfy each other's sexual needs, but they are also able to satisfy the higher, more important needs of self-esteem and value. . . .

Here again is what I want in my life: I want to make love to my husband because I cherish and respect who he is and not just because I want sex. And I want a husband who makes love to me for the same reasons. I want a husband that I can grow old with; and when sex may not be good anymore, I believe God will bless our union with even greater pleasures—pleasures that have lasting value. . . .

Only you can choose what you want out of life; you have always had free will and you still do. I already know what I want and I hope you understand that I can't accept less. Now I guess we have to decide if our desires match.

I chose you as my husband a long time ago, but maybe you never chose me to be your wife. You have to choose now. And if your choice hurts, we'll live through it.

You told me that one of the values you still hold dear is freedom. Somehow, I can't help but believe that you're struggling with freedom of choice. That's one human trait that God will not control; and you're right when you say you have to figure it out alone.

You and I both are ashamed of the choices you've made in the past year, Ricky. But today offers a new life, and you can choose to live with self-respect and value and do the very best you can do. That might even mean letting me go. Maybe you should . . . maybe you shouldn't. Only God knows that. Even when we try to do our best, we still make *mistakes. The important thing is that we've got to respect ourselves, accept the consequences, and know we tried our best.*

Ricky, I don't want your love because of obligation or shame. I don't need it and I deserve better. Love from you has got to come from your freedom of choice.

> *Love,*
> *Bettye*

When she had finished the letter, Bettye telephoned Ricky on the road and said, "I've written you a letter. It tells you how I feel about our marriage and what I expect from you. I just wanted to let you know I'm putting it in the mail tomorrow."

"Okay, Bettye. Good. Listen, I want you to Federal Express it to me. I'll get it sooner."

"All right, Ricky. I'll do that." As she hung up the phone, she thought, *Wow! What I think still matters to him.*

The next day, after she'd mailed the letter, Bettye received a phone call from Linda Thompson. "Since our talk the other day I've been thinking a lot about you," Linda told her. "It looks to me like everything in your life lately is snowballing into a major nightmare."

"That's just how I've been feeling," Bettye agreed.

"Well, I think you need to get away for a few days, so I've decided we're going on a trip."

"*You've* decided?" Bettye chuckled. "Where are we going, Linda?"

"I don't know. I figured we'd just get in the car and head south."

"How far south do you suppose I'll need to go to get away from my problems?"

"Probably the South Pole, but I'm not that ambitious. I was thinking more like Panama City Beach."

"It sounds super, Linda, but I really don't see how I can go. I'm taking classes full time, you know."

"And I know next week is your spring break. We'll just go for a few days, Bettye. You need a change of scene. How about it—just the two of us gals hitting the road for some fun in the sun?"

"Sure. Why not? I'll even drive, if you like."

"Great. I'll meet you Monday afternoon at your townhouse."

After hanging up with Linda, Bettye telephoned Ricky. "I just wanted to let you know Linda and I are going away for a few days. I just feel like I really need to get away."

"Okay. Say, I got a great idea, Bettye. I know just where you two should go." He suggested a certain Gulf Coast town.

"Why?"

"Because it's so pretty down there. I had a few concerts there a while back. You'll really like it, Bettye. Why don't you go there?"

"Well, okay, Ricky. If you say so."

On Monday, as they packed their luggage in the trunk of Bettye's Pontiac Bonneville, she told Linda about the town Ricky had suggested. "He says it's real pretty, so I told him we'd go there."

Linda looked skeptical. "You sure he said it's pretty there?"

"He said it's pretty."

"Okay, here we go. And it sure better be pretty!"

They got a later start than they had planned, so it was nearly midnight when they finally turned off the interstate and entered the city limits. Bettye was already wishing she could crawl into her own bed back home, but right now even a hotel bed would look good. "Which hotel are we staying at?" she asked Linda.

"I don't know, Bettye. Which one did you make reservations at?"

Bettye heaved a sigh. "I never thought about reservations!"

"That's okay," said Linda. "How hard can it be to find a hotel room this time of year?"

"Look, there's a Best Western right up the road," said Bettye. "We'll check there."

"Don't bother. The 'No Vacancy' sign is on."

"All right. I see another one a few blocks down. I'm sure they'll have a room."

They tried every hotel in a two-mile radius. Not one had a vacancy. "What'd Ricky do?" asked Linda. "Tell the whole world to come here this week?"

"I should have made reservations," Bettye lamented.

"Don't despair. We'll find a place yet." Linda squinted in the darkness, trying to read her *AAA Tour Book*. "They should print these in Day-Glo so a person could read them."

"Wait, Linda. I see a place up ahead. There, on the right. Isn't that a motel?"

Linda peered out her side window. "I don't know, Bettye. It looks kind of small and drab to me."

"Well, it looks beautiful to me," said Bettye. "The sign says *'Vacancy'*!"

175

S H E   S T A Y S

Linda nodded. "Yeah, right! I can see why there's a vacancy."

In spite of their misgivings, they wasted no time in securing a room. With overnight bags in tow, they made their way through the darkness until they found the door bearing their room number. Linda unlocked the door and they stepped into a dreary cubicle offering sagging twin beds, utilitarian night stands, a broken TV, and gray walls with faded prints by an unknown artist.

"It's not exactly the Ritz," said Linda.

Bettye sighed. "It's not even the Salvation Army. I said I needed to get away from it all, but not this far!"

Linda opened a drawer. "At least it's not uncharted territory. The Gideons have been here before us. Besides, we're just going to sleep. How bad can it be?"

They found out soon enough. Minutes after they had turned off the light and climbed into their beds, Bettye became aware of something—a sound, a presence; she couldn't pinpoint it, but she knew they weren't alone. "Do you hear something?" she whispered.

"What? The patter of little feet?" quipped Linda.

"Not exactly. Just a scratchy, rustling sound." She reached out, turned on the gooseneck lamp over the bed, and gazed at the floor in time to see several large shiny black cockroaches scurrying across the floor. "Oh, Linda, it's *lots* of little feet!"

Linda sat up and drew her covers up around her neck. "We're safe, as long as we stay in bed. By morning they'll have all gone home!"

"That's just where I want to be," cried Bettye.

"I promise, tomorrow will be a better day."

Bettye pulled the covers over her head. "Yeah, I've heard that before too!"

The next morning, as a salmon-pink sun seeped in through the venetian blinds, Bettye and Linda climbed out of their beds and stepped gingerly over the worn carpet, dodging any lingering roaches. "Look, we have a balcony," said Linda, opening the sliding glass door.

"And look, there's a swimming pool down there!" said Bettye.

They slipped out onto the tiny balcony and gazed down. Linda clasped her hand over her mouth. "Ugh! The whole pool is covered with black grunge!"

Bettye turned away. "It's filthy! Disgusting!"

"Maybe we didn't choose the right hotel," said Linda with a wry note of whimsy.

"We didn't choose it; it chose us," said Bettye as they went back inside. "It was the only place nobody else wanted."

"I think they made a movie about this motel," mused Linda, "and what happened to the guests wasn't good."

"You don't have to convince me. Let's get out of here."

"First, let's take a walk on the beach. The scenery should be breathtaking."

They put on T-shirts, shorts, and tennis shoes; Bettye ran a brush through her thick auburn curls and Linda quickly combed her short bob. With high hopes they started out for the beach. They walked along a meandering path, then crossed a little bridge, and made their way onto the hard-packed sand. "It smells bad," said Bettye, wrinkling her nose. "Like a sewer."

"Like dead fish," said Linda, stepping over random patches of litter, bottles, and cans.

Bettye sidestepped a black tarlike substance that marred the beach as far as her eye could see. "Maybe it's a bad tide day."

"Is that anything like a bad hair day?"

They walked on for about ten minutes, too absorbed in watching their step to engage in conversation. Suddenly Bettye realized Linda was no longer beside her. She stopped and looked around. Linda was standing ten feet behind, her arms folded, her eyebrows raised. Round-faced and salt-of-the-earth practical, Linda always seemed to exude maternal wisdom. "Um, Bettye?" she said, drawing out each syllable.

"You want to leave, don't you, Linda?"

"Do you want to stay?"

"No! Let's go!"

"Yes! Let's go *now*!"

They took off running like schoolgirls just released from class. They hurried back to their motel room, gathered their things, checked out, and jumped into Bettye's Bonneville with huge sighs of relief. And laughter!

"And this was supposed to be our great little getaway," said Bettye as she pulled away from the motel.

"Maybe the rest of this town is gorgeous," said Linda, "but *we're* not going to hang around to find out!"

As Bettye merged with early morning traffic, she glanced over quizzically at Linda. "So where are we going now?"

"I don't know. Where do you want to go?"

"How about Panama City Beach?"

"That's where we were going in the first place."

"Yeah, before Ricky said, 'Come to this little town, because it's so beautiful.'" Bettye shook her head and laughed. "Boy, is Ricky in the dark, or what?"

Linda laughed too. And then the underlying irony struck them both. "Ricky's so blinded right now he can't even recognize the difference between beauty and filth!"

They drove all morning, taking the interstate that paralleled the coast to Florida, then followed US-98 into a resort town named Destin. The scenery was exquisite.

In Destin, Bettye caught a glimpse of a plush Hilton Hotel in the distance. She looked at Linda. "We haven't reached Panama City Beach yet, but I'm tired of driving. What about stopping here?"

"Let's—if they have a room. It looks fantastic."

At the front desk, Bettye said, "I want something really luxurious. The best you've got. We feel like being pampered."

The room clerk showed them to an elegant suite with a living room and two spacious bedrooms. "This is the most beautiful place I've ever seen," Bettye exclaimed. "And, boy, do we deserve it!"

Linda sat down on the plush sofa. "Right! We deserve a real treat. And that's what we're going to have!"

Behaving like true tourists, they took leisurely walks on a snow-white beach and gazed out at a spangling, emerald-green ocean; they received rejuvenating body massages at the resort next door; they dined on succulent lobster and steak at the posh Elephant Walk restaurant; and they slept the deep, unruffled slumber of indulged, mollycoddled children.

They left the next day and headed back to Nashville, feeling refreshed, energized, and wonderfully content.

Just outside of Mobile, Alabama, Linda suggested, "Let's stop at Bellingrath Gardens. The flowers are absolutely beautiful."

Bettye agreed, reluctant to let their glorious vacation come to an end. "I've heard of these gardens. Weren't they built by a wealthy couple who had no children?"

"Yes. The couple were so in love, they dedicated their lives to cultivating acres and acres of beautiful flowers."

For several hours Bettye and Linda strolled through Bellingrath Gardens—eight hundred magnificent acres skirting the Isle-aux-Oies River, replete with brilliant blossoms, exotic flowers, landscaped lakes, lush fountains, cascades, and sparkling waterfalls. As they walked, their senses were pleasantly assaulted by the combined fragrances of over 250,000 blooming azaleas and purple hyacinths; it was a heady, intoxicating perfume.

"Can you believe it?" said Linda. "Some of these azaleas are over a hundred years old!"

Bettye shook her head with a reverent awe. "Imagine the love these two people shared, which created and sustained this marvelous place!" What she couldn't put into words was that these gardens spoke to the deep need in her heart for permanence and stability in her own life. Would she ever experience such profound and enduring love?

Even after Bettye arrived home that afternoon, the balm and beauty of the gardens lingered in her thoughts. She was grateful to God for this tranquil interlude; she felt more at peace than she had in months.

But it was the peace before the storm—the calm before another shattering event that would drive her to the point of losing her mind.

CHAPTER 19

*B*ettye stopped by her townhouse only long enough to drop Linda off to pick up her car and to unpack a few of her own belongings. Then she headed out to the farm to collect the mail, pay some bills, and do some laundry. She was wearing the same white short-sleeved blouse and white shorts she had worn on her trip home.

To her surprise, Ricky was outside in his work clothes, walking around the front yard. The breeze was sweet and clean, gently ruffling her hair, and the grass was turning a verdant green. The flower beds were already alive with color; purple, yellow, and white crocuses were in full bloom, and daffodils—those pretty little yellow buttercups—were just starting to blossom. With the loveliness of the Bellingrath Gardens still fresh in her mind, Bettye noted that this was a perfect scene—her handsome husband and her own lovely home and gardens waiting for her. Yes, spring was in the air, bringing new life and hope.

Bettye said hello and fell into step beside Ricky; she relished moments like this; they were all too few these days. At least he didn't seem edgy around her lately, neither did he avoid her gaze or pretend she wasn't there as he had in the past.

As they walked, he asked about her trip and she told him of her wonderful time with Linda. She discreetly avoided mentioning the 'beautiful' town he had recommended. "Would you believe?" she went on brightly, "Linda and Jerry are turning right around tomorrow and driving back down to Panama Beach. They have a trailer and will be spending the rest of the week there soaking up the sun."

Ricky nodded. "Yeah, I remember they had a trailer there."

They walked on in companionable silence. Finally Bettye asked with forced nonchalance, "Did you get my letter?"

He glanced over at her, his expression inscrutable. "Yeah, Bettye. I did. Thanks."

She waited for him to say more, and when he didn't, she resisted the urge to ask. It had to mean he hadn't made his decision yet. "So when are you leaving?" she asked instead.

"Tomorrow."

"Where's your bus?"

"In Nashville. My driver will swing by for me in the morning."

"You have just one concert?"

"Yeah. Just one this time, and another one next week."

"So I guess you'll be back home day after tomorrow?"

He didn't answer right away. When he did reply, Bettye detected several layers of meaning in his tone. "I'm not coming back this time, Bettye," he said solemnly. "I'm gonna stay out on the road."

She stared at him in bewilderment. "Why? You'll have several free days between concerts. What are you going to do with all that free time?"

He turned his gaze away from her. "I'm gonna find out once and for all what kind of life I want."

She felt her blood turn cold. "What are you talking about?"

"I guess you might as well know. I'm gonna be hitting some towns where there will be lots of available women at my beck and call." He drew in a sharp breath. "I'm gonna spend some time in those towns and find out whether I still wanna be with those women or not."

A knot of fear tightened in her throat. "Wait a minute, Ricky! You're going to go be with those women?"

He cast her a quick glance. "I don't know what I'm gonna do, Bettye, but I know I gotta be out there to find out."

They had walked the length of the driveway and arrived at the small log cabin Ricky had transported log by log to this site a year ago. It was a frontier cabin over 150 years old, primitive, with log walls, beams of roughhewn timber, and a gray stone fireplace. Ricky loved his little pioneer cabin and spent hours here whenever he could find the time. She and Ricky had even slept in the cabin's cedar log bed he had framed with ropes and pegs instead of nails.

They went inside and sat down in the two antique rocking chairs that faced the rock fireplace. The air was damp and cold and the light thin and pale. Bettye felt the coldness worming its way into her heart. "Ricky, this isn't fair," she protested."It's not a fair test!"

He ran his hand over the round log table that stood between their chairs. He had cut the slab from an old maple tree. "What are you talking about? What's not fair?"

"I can't compete with these mysterious women with their little love games. I don't have a chance!"

"What do you mean—you don't have a chance?"

Desperation rose in her throat like gall. "I can't win! You're going to choose them; I know it!"

He scowled. "How do you know that? I don't even know."

The words tumbled out, her voice high and strangled. "What chance do I have? With me, all you have are responsibilities and obligations, bills and pressures. I'm thirty-eight years old, Ricky. We've been together for over twelve years. I'm not new anymore. There's nothing exciting about me anymore."

"That's not so—"

She clasped his arm. "It is, Ricky. These women you're putting me up against—they have no strings attached. They love to party. When you're with them, you can be free and laugh and have fun and not think about ties. They're beautiful and young and free-spirited and happy-go-lucky; they don't have wrinkles."

Tears rolled down her cheeks. "Please don't put me up against these women, Ricky."

A tendon in his neck throbbed and his eyes darkened into black coals. "I've got to find out, Bettye. Do you understand? I've got to go find out."

She raked her fingers through her thick russet hair. "You don't have to go. I already know the answer!"

He pivoted in his chair to face her. "How can you know the answer when I don't know the answer?"

She buried her face in her hands. She was weeping uncontrollably now. "What chance do I have, Ricky? What chance do I have?"

"That's what I've got to find out." He stood up and walked to the door. His voice was sharp and hard as flint. "I can't take this, Bettye. I'm leaving now. I'm going back to the house to call my driver and tell him to come get me. I'll spend the night in Nashville on the bus."

As he stalked out of the cabin, she scrambled out of her chair and followed him into the late afternoon sunlight. She blinked against the glare. A pounding had started behind her eyes and the pain was snaking around her skull like tentacles, short-circuiting her thoughts.

Ricky was already taking long strides up the driveway toward the house. She ran after him and grabbed the back of his shirt and wrapped her arms around his strapping frame. "Don't go, Ricky. Don't do this," she begged, pressing her wet face against his back. "I can't stand it anymore!"

He seized her hands and broke her hold, then wheeled around to face her, gripping her wrists. "I've got to do this, Bettye. Do you hear me? We will never know— *I* will never know, *you* will never know until I do this!"

He released her wrists and turned away, but she flung out her arms again and clutched his shirt tail. He gave a sudden wrenching lurch, freeing himself, and marched on up to the house without a backward glance.

Bettye fell to her knees and collapsed prostrate on the

driveway, sobbing, the gravel digging into her bare arms and legs. "Ricky, please don't do this to me! Don't go!"

She cried until her chest heaved with dry sobs. Then she stood up shakily, brushed the debris from her limbs, and plodded to the house. She went directly upstairs to her room and dropped into bed. She lay weeping for what seemed hours, until hiccups and exhaustion replaced her tears, and darkness began absorbing the waning daylight.

Sometime just before dusk she heard the bus pull up. Minutes later she heard Ricky leave—the front door slammed; he never said good-bye or called up to her or looked in on her. The bus trundled away, leaving her alone in a house filled with silence.

She lay still in her high-posted, tiger oak bed, listening to the sound of her own breathing, as deepening shadows crept over the room. One wall of the huge bedroom was composed entirely of windows and glass French doors that opened on a glassed-in balcony. The final remnants of daylight filtered through the mini-blinds and streamed across one wall displaying a framed cross-stitch embroidered with her name and Ricky's and their wedding date.

On the same wall was an old painting Ricky had bought for her in an antique store. It showed a beautiful guardian angel watching over a small girl and her little brother as they crossed a dangerous foot bridge during a storm over a raging creek. Ricky had grown up with a smaller replica of the painting in his bedroom; they had both always been captivated by it and were delighted when Ricky found the larger print for their home. To Bettye it had symbolized angels watching over her and Ricky and their marriage.

Where were her angels now?

She closed her eyes against the darkness, too weary even to reach out to turn on a lamp. On the screen of her mind she saw her husband—his bronzed skin, his virile, earthy good looks, his smoky green eyes. She could hear his voice in her head—the mellow, sensual tones as he whispered words of love. But he wasn't whispering to her; in her mind's eye she saw him laughing and drinking beer with a beautiful, supple young woman! To her horror she saw them embracing, making love.

She pressed her palms against her eyes to block out the images. But as quickly as one vanished, another took its place, revealing Ricky with another woman even younger and prettier than the one before. Every vile deed Ricky had described during his confession flashed before her now in vivid, mocking, devastating detail.

She rolled over and buried her face in her hands. "No, take it away!" she cried. She struggled to turn her mind to other thoughts, but it was useless. The visions continued to assault her, one after another showing Ricky with all his other women.

For hours she tossed and turned as the scenes played in her imagination, tormentingly graphic. The effort of banishing them from her mind left her weak, her skin wet with perspiration. "I've got to get some sleep," she wailed. "I keep trying, but, oh, Lord, I can't sleep!"

She turned over on her back and stared up into the shadows at the beadboard ceiling with its huge beams. She could feel her heart pounding under her ribs—a persistent throbbing like the ache behind her eyes. "Dear God, why don't You just take me home and let it end here!" she said aloud. "I can't stand this horrible torment. I've got to find relief. I'm going to go crazy."

She closed her eyes, feverish, the warm moisture beading on her forehead and around her neck. *Oh, Lord, is this what it's like to go crazy? Am I losing my sanity? Am I too far over the edge to go back?*

Into the darkness she whispered, "Jesus, dear Jesus, I've got to have some rest. Lord Jesus, give me rest!" For several moments she continued to murmur, "Jesus . . . Jesus . . . Jesus."

Then, as she lay on her bed with her eyes closed, she felt a cool, smooth, comforting hand on her forehead. She didn't open her eyes; she knew it was Jesus. She felt His presence, His peace. She heard Him say, "Rest, My child."

And then His hand moved across her brow, and peace swept over her like a cooling river washing away the pain. Incredibly, all the ugliness was gone—the nightmarish images, the torment, the despair; everything was gone except the deep, sweet, satisfying peace of her Savior—the same peace the little boy and girl must have known in her guardian angel painting.

"Thank You, Jesus!" She turned over, pulled her covers up around her, and slipped into the most peaceful, restful sleep she had ever known.

CHAPTER 20

*B*ettye woke the next morning feeling rested. Sunlight streamed in through the windows, filling the room with brightness and warmth. A tickle of joy went through her as she thought about last night's miracle. That's what it was—a miracle! Only God—through Christ's healing touch—could have turned her emotions around so dramatically, taking her from the edge of hysteria and despair to absolute, unshakable peace.

The tranquillity remained even as she thought about Ricky beginning his trip today and carrying out his dreadful test. She realized there was no way she could stay at home, pacing the floor, waiting to hear what his decision would be. She needed something to occupy her mind, and she needed to be with someone who could pray with her for Ricky. She thought of Andy, but this was Easter weekend and Andy wasn't available. Then she thought of Linda.

As soon as she had dressed Bettye telephoned Linda and said, "I really need to get away again for a few days. Would you and Jerry like some company on your trip to Florida? You would? Great! I'm still packed from our trip, so I can be ready when you get here. Ricky? He's gone again. It's a long story, but I'll explain everything when I see you."

Minutes later, as she set her sweater and overnight bag by the front door, Bettye glanced around with a tug of nostalgia at the large entryway that had become a storage room for Ricky's cherished mementos—his big flashy jukeboxes, his massive hand-carved oak bar from an English pub, his old-fashioned upright piano, his thirties-style white enamel stove and linoleum kitchen table. Ricky was in every timber and trinket in this house, just as he was in her every heartbeat.

No! I can't think about Ricky, she chided herself. *Not today!*

As she watched out the front window for the Thompsons' car, she noticed Ricky's bus pulling up in the driveway. "That's strange," she murmured. "I figured he would've been on the road hours ago."

She went out onto the porch and down the steps and waited a moment as he got off the bus and started toward her. She met him in the yard and instinctively put her arms around him and hugged him tight. She could feel him hugging her back. They remained in a close embrace for what seemed a very long time.

Finally he stepped back and looked at her with a deep, perplexed scrutiny. She could read the worry in his eyes. *He came back because he's worried about me!*

"Are you all right?" he asked.

"Yes, Ricky, I'm fine. What are you doing here?"

"I, um, I forgot something. Nothin' real important, just—if you're okay, I'll just run in and get it."

"Sure, Ricky." She clasped his arm. "I . . . I'm

sorry for the way I acted last night. I was wrong. I want you to know I understand why you have to go. And I want you to know I'm going to be praying for you while you're gone."

He looked baffled, but relieved. "Thanks, Bettye. Listen, you take care of yourself." He hugged her again. "And I'll call you . . . as soon as I know."

She looked up at him. "Ricky, I'm leaving too. I can't stay here waiting and wondering. I'm going with Linda and Jerry to Panama Beach for the weekend. We'll be staying in their trailer. I'll get you the number."

"Okay. Like I said, I'll call when I—"

"I know, Ricky. I'll be waiting to hear from you."

Shortly after his bus drove off down the road, Jerry and Linda Thompson arrived in their big white Buick. As Jerry loaded her luggage in the trunk Bettye knew this trip was just what she needed. Nobody was better at taking a person's mind off her troubles than Jerry, with his steady stream of jokes and stories.

And Linda was always ready with a comforting hug, a prayer, or a word of encouragement. Plus, they both loved Ricky.

The weekend passed quickly enough, considering that Bettye was waiting for a decision that would determine her entire future. She relaxed and spent hours chatting with Jerry and Linda in their homey trailer nestled in a secluded glen among towering trees. On Saturday she and Linda got up early and walked on the beach and sat for hours on the rippling sand dunes, talking and praying.

On Easter morning they rose before dawn and drove around Panama City looking for a church to attend.

When they happened by a little church on Jenks Street, Bettye said, "Wait! That's the church!"

Linda looked at her. "Why? What's so special about that one?"

"It's on Jenks Street. That's the name of Ricky's daddy."

They both began to laugh. "By all means," said Linda, "what better place could we be on Easter Sunday than Jenks Street?"

The two of them attended the sunrise service at the plain little church. As the first vivid streamers of light chased away the darkness Bettye welcomed these serene moments to worship and offer praise to her risen Savior. Still, uppermost in her mind was the disquieting fact that this was Ricky's first free day on the road. Would he be spending today with some other woman?

Doing their best to keep Bettye's mind off Ricky, Jerry and Linda took her to visit a friend who lived on a houseboat. They spent Sunday afternoon laughing and relaxing in good company. The diversion worked to a degree, even though Ricky was never far from Bettye's thoughts.

That evening, shortly after they arrived back at the trailer, the phone rang. Linda answered and handed the phone to Bettye. "It's Ricky."

She took the receiver with trembling fingers. "Hello, Ricky. Happy Easter."

"Thanks, Bettye. Happy Easter to you too."

"I didn't think I'd hear from you today."

He came right to the point. "Bettye, I've made my decision."

SHELTON & LANDIS

Her heart started pounding, but she forced her voice to remain calm. "Okay, Ricky."

"I don't want the other women. I want to see if I can be a husband to you."

"Oh, Ricky!" She steadied herself; her legs felt weak.

"But, Bettye, I need time. I don't know yet if I can pull myself back. I just don't know yet. But I know now that I don't need these other women. I know that. I will not see them. Let's not talk about divorce right now. I don't know if I'll be able to do this, Bettye, but I know I want to try."

"Okay, Ricky, we'll start again." Her hopes soared, but she knew he still wasn't committing himself to being a husband again. He wasn't saying, *We'll get back together and fall into each other's arms and live happily ever after.* He was really saying, *I'll stay away from other women until I find out if I can be happy with you.* She understood that; she wouldn't entertain false expectations.

"Ricky, what if you start drinking and get drunk again?"

"Bettye, I've got to be able to get a handle on that, I've got to," he said fervently. "And I'm telling you I'm going to do my best. If it happens, you'll be the first to know. I will never lie to you again."

"All right, Ricky. Thank you. This is a big step you're taking."

When Bettye returned from Panama Beach the next day, she went back to her townhouse. She knew Ricky wasn't ready for her to move back to the farm. But that was all right. She felt good again, strong, confident, and protected by God.

She realized with relief that her negative feelings that

day at the cabin weren't valid; in fact, those lies had almost destroyed her. She knew now she *could* compete with younger, prettier women for Ricky's love. *Those other women don't have a chance against me because I know Ricky for who he really is. I know him inside and out. I know all the bad things about him and all the good things. I'm the one who has true love to give him, not them. They love him because he's a superstar. I love him because he's a man. With me, all I ask him to be is himself. I'm the one he can grow old with, and I'll be the one to take care of him when he's sick. He doesn't know it yet, but those "chicks" don't have a chance!*

Two days later, on a sunny spring morning, Ricky phoned Bettye at the townhouse and said, "I just finished talking to my dad."

"You did? Your dad? You called him?"

"Yeah."

"Why did you call him?"

Ricky's voice was solemn, matter-of-fact. "I told him, Bettye."

"Ricky, you told your dad?"

"I told him everything."

"Oh, Ricky, why? We've been so careful not to let anyone in the family know."

"Bettye, I just had to have some help. I had to talk to somebody." He sounded weary, an edge of desperation in his tone. "I've been trying to talk to God. I've been talking and talking, but He doesn't answer. He's not even listening. I had to ask somebody to help me. I couldn't think of anyone else except my daddy."

Bettye's thoughts raced. Jenks Shelton did not have a

strong heart; he had already had by-pass surgery and a couple of heart attacks. "Is your father okay?"

"I guess so."

"What did he say?"

"He didn't say anything for a long time, and I said, 'Daddy, tell me what to do.' Finally, the only thing Daddy said was, 'You better pray, Son.' I said, 'I've been praying, but I'm not getting any answers.' Daddy just said, 'Then you ain't prayed hard enough.' I said, 'Daddy, I want you to tell me what to do!' But Daddy just said there wasn't any more he could tell me. Bettye, he didn't want to talk to me anymore."

Bettye winced at the pain in Ricky's voice. She yearned to reach out and comfort him. For the first time he'd reached out, and been rejected. "Ricky, it's just because you caught him off-guard. How could you expect him to know what to say? Don't be too hard on him."

"Bettye, I just needed to talk to my daddy, and he couldn't help me."

Hearing Ricky's anguish gave her a ray of hope. *Thank God, something is happening in his heart. Always before he said, "I've got to do it on my own." For the first time he's admitting he needs help!* "Ricky," she said, "I've got to call and see if your mom and dad are all right."

"Don't worry, Bettye. He's not gonna tell my mom. He promised he wouldn't tell Mama."

After hanging up the phone, Bettye couldn't get Ricky's parents off her mind. *I'll call them anyway,* she decided, *just to make sure everything's okay.* But the moment Bettye heard Eloise's voice and asked how things were, she knew Jenks—"Whick," to his wife—had told her.

"Oh, Bettye, things aren't good."

"What's wrong, Eloise?" she asked warily.

The anguished words spilled out. "What are we going to do, Bettye? Whick told me everything!"

"What do you mean, what are we going to do?" said Bettye. "You know what we're going to do. We're going to stand by Ricky."

Eloise went on hopelessly, as if she hadn't heard her. "I can't believe it, Bettye. I can't believe my son would do something like this. It's so sorry; it's so low down!"

"Eloise," Bettye said firmly, "you know Ricky is a good man. He's going through a hard time right now. We've got to pray for him. He's going to get through this. Don't you give up on him."

"Bettye, thank God you're standing by him!"

"I am, Eloise. Now let me talk to Jenks."

When he got on the phone, she said, "Jenks, you know Ricky didn't want you to tell Eloise. You know she won't be able to handle this."

"I had to tell somebody," he said, the emotion heavy in his voice. "If Ricky thought I could carry this on my own shoulders, I can't. I had to turn to somebody, and I turned to my wife."

"Jenks, you believe God can turn Ricky around, don't you?"

The words came out in a sob. "I know He can."

"So all we have to do is pray together. We've got to have faith, believe in God, and believe the goodness in Ricky is still there."

"I want to, Bettye."

"You know this isn't the real Ricky. We've got to keep

196

praying for the real Ricky to come back. He's going to come back, Jenks."

His voice broke, but there was a glimmer of hope. "I know he is, Bettye."

"And we're going to be strong for him. We're going to get through this. Now that you know, I have more prayer warriors."

"You sure do, Bettye. Don't give up on our boy. We're all gonna be praying for him."

After talking with Ricky's parents, Bettye called Ricky back. "I just want you to know your mom and dad are going to be okay."

"My mom?"

"Yeah, your dad had to tell her."

"Oh, good grief, Bettye, not Mama! She'll never understand!"

"Your daddy didn't have a choice. He needed somebody and he turned to his wife. It was the only thing for him to do."

"Oh, not Mama," he wailed, "not my mama!"

Bettye could feel her own heart breaking with Ricky's. "Listen, Ricky, I've got to talk to my mom and dad. Now that your parents know, I've got to tell mine. I can't let them hear this from anyone other than me."

"I understand, Bettye."

She called her parents that same day. "Can you come to the farmhouse?" she asked. "I need to talk to you."

They lived eight hours away in Virginia, but her mother didn't even ask what she wanted; she just said, "We'll be there as soon as we can."

They arrived the next day. Bettye met them at the farmhouse, but she waited until the next day, after they had settled in, before telling them about Ricky. The three of them were sitting in rocking chairs on the front porch enjoying the fresh air and spring blossoms when Bettye said, "Mom and Dad, I've got something to tell you."

They were sitting at an angle from her, so she was able to see their grave expressions. They knew something was wrong, but they remained silent, giving her time to collect her thoughts. She could hear birds chirping overhead and leaves rustling in the breeze. The beefalo were grazing in the pasture and the sky was as bright a blue as she'd ever seen. Quietly she said, "I'm not sure if Ricky and I will be able to stay married."

They continued rocking in their chairs, waiting, letting her have her say. It seemed even the birds stopped singing as she said in a gentle, straightforward voice, "Ricky has started drinking real heavy, and he's lost control of himself. When he's been drunk, he's been with some other women, and now we're waiting to see if we're going to be able to make our marriage work or not."

She could see tears glisten in her mother's eyes. A rush of emotion choked her own words. "I just need you to know it's a possibility it may not work out. I wanted you to hear it from me."

They were both so quiet she wondered for a moment if they had understood what she was telling them. Finally her mother reached across to her chair and squeezed her hand. "Bettye," she said unflinchingly, "you need to stand by Ricky."

Bettye felt a wave of relief sweep over her. "I know, Mom."

Her father sat forward and looked her in the eye. "Bettye, he'll get over this. Ricky will come back. Men sometimes make mistakes, Bettye. I know what it's like for Ricky to be away from home so much. Living on the road is a hard life. I used to travel for a living, so I know. Ricky is going to snap out of this. You need to stand by him."

Tears rolled down Bettye's cheeks. "I know, Daddy. I believe that with all my heart. I just need you to help me pray for him."

"We'll pray for both of you," her mother said staunchly. Her eyes narrowed and grew as hard as ball bearings. "Bettye, don't you dare let those other women take your husband away from you!"

Bettye chuckled in spite of herself. "Mama, I'm doing my best. I'm doing my best!"

The three of them stood up at the same time. Bettye kissed and hugged each one, and thanked them. "You're the greatest parents in the world!" She was so proud of the way they had reacted. "I needed you to feel this way," she said through her tears. "I needed to hear you say these things and back me up, because I am going to stand by my husband."

CHAPTER 21

On Easter Sunday, as Bettye felt a glimmer of hope over Ricky's decision to give up other women, Andy was about to face a Waterloo of sorts with Steve. She had just spent a week in Los Angeles filming a television commercial, and now, on Easter night, she was flying back to Nashville. Steve would be waiting to pick her up at the airport.

Andy's week in L.A. had given her the physical and emotional distance from Steve to gain some perspective about their relationship. Her soul-searching had brought her to one conclusion—she must break up with Steve completely. And she would do it tonight.

Surely it was time. For weeks, if not months, their relationship had been deteriorating; their time together lately was marked either by bitter arguments or cold silences; their conversations were filled with anger and blame; their love was riddled with pain.

Andy was convinced that Steve saw her friendship with Bettye as a betrayal. And perhaps it was. Perhaps she was being more loyal to her friend than to her fiancé. But what else could she do? She was only following God's leading.

She had not worn Steve's engagement ring for weeks now, knowing their future was on hold. But how long could she let things drift before she made a decisive move?

In Los Angeles she had prayed with several girlfriends for God's direction in her life. Now, as the plane carried her back to Nashville, she felt stronger and more confident than she had in weeks. God was about to do something significant. She sensed it. If Steve wasn't the man for her, there would be someone better. She had been holding on so tight; she had felt so torn and guilty over not being all that Steve needed. Now it was time to let him go once and for all.

It's time I do for myself what I've encouraged Bettye to do for herself—think about who I am as a woman, what I've accomplished, and what my dreams are. Last year at this time I confronted cancer and my own mortality; this year I'm faced with losing Steve. I survived then; I'll survive now. I don't want to live with anger and pain and blame. I'm not a status quo person; I want to knock down walls and be passionate and be the best I can be. I have a lot to offer the right man. If Steve can't see that, then he's not the man for me.

When Andy stepped off the plane in Nashville and spotted Steve waiting for her, looking tall and handsome and masterful, she wondered if she would waver in her decision to let him go. But no, it was settled. In fact, now that the burden of indecision was lifted, she was happy to see him. And he seemed genuinely pleased to see her. Even as they embraced and he gathered her luggage and

201

walked her to his car, she felt that she had made the right choice.

Strangely, Steve himself seemed different, less angry, more relaxed and congenial. Perhaps he already sensed the change in her. As he chatted about work and the weather and what had happened in Nashville during her absence, she thought, *You don't even realize it, Steve, but I've already let you go. I release you to discover what God has for you. I want you to be happy and find the right person, someone who can be to you all the things I can't be.*

As Steve drove her back to his house so that they could spend the last few hours of Easter together, Andy wondered, *Do I dare break up with him on Easter? Should I wait until tomorrow?* But no. She had made her decision. It was time to let Steve know she wouldn't be marrying him.

The mood was so mellow and the evening so pleasant. They were sitting on the comfortable sofa in his living room, the lamplight diffusing a rosy glow. "Big Band" jazz from the forties was playing on the stereo—Glenn Miller, Tommy Dorsey, Benny Goodman. She found it ironic that she felt closer to Steve now than she had in weeks.

Steve's cat, Tommy, padded over and rubbed against her leg. She scooped him up on her lap and began petting him the way she often did. She couldn't imagine any animal being loved more than Steve loved this cat, except for maybe his dog, Danny. She had spent so much time in Steve's house, she felt as if Tommy and Danny were hers, too.

As she massaged Tommy's neck, Andy silently composed the words she would say to Steve to end their relationship. At last she steeled herself and began, speaking with a quiet precision. "Steve, I have something important to tell you. I've been thinking about it for a long time, but it wasn't until I was in Los Angeles this past week that everything crystallized for me, and I know now what I have to—"

She paused and picked Tommy up in both hands.

Steve frowned. "What's the matter?"

She ran her fingers along Tommy's rib cage. "Something's wrong with Tommy."

He reached over and scratched Tommy's ears. "What do you mean, something's wrong? He seems okay to me."

"Hold him, Steve. Don't you feel it? He's nothing but skin and bones and fur."

Steve lifted the cat up in his arms and felt along Tommy's ribs. "You're right, Andy. When did he get so skinny?"

"You probably wouldn't notice; you're with him all the time, but I haven't seen him for over a week."

"I'd better take him to the vet tomorrow. Will you come with us, Andy?"

She gazed at Steve, at the urgent, little-boy look in a face usually marked by imposing dignity. "Sure, I'll go with you." She settled back against his shoulder and listened to Tommy purr contentedly in his arms. *I'd better wait until we're sure Tommy's got a clean bill of health before I break up with Steve,* she decided.

But the next day, the news from the vet wasn't good. "Your cat has cancer," he said matter-of-factly. "Feline leukemia. He probably won't live."

Steve looked stricken. "Isn't there something you can do?"

"We could perform emergency surgery and remove the tumor, but I can't offer much hope."

Andy looked up at Steve and clasped his hand. "We've got to try. Tommy's a member of the family."

He nodded. "If there's the slightest chance, go ahead. We'll do whatever it takes to save him."

The veterinarian arched one bristly brow and cleared his throat as he jotted something on Tommy's chart. "All right. We'll schedule him for first thing tomorrow morning. Take him home now, but don't give him any food or water. Bring him back at eight sharp."

On the way home, Andy held Tommy and nuzzled the top of his velvety head with her chin. While Tommy purred happily, she and Steve remained silent. Steve didn't speak until they were driving through downtown Nashville. Suddenly he pointed at one of the towering buildings and said, "Look, they have the big sign up again for the Sara Lee Golf Tournament. It was up there just like that last year when we found out you had that malignant melanoma."

Andy nodded. She remembered the sign. She recalled thinking that people were getting excited about golf when she didn't know if she'd be alive next month or next year.

"I was so scared," Steve said quietly. "I never prayed so hard in my life."

"Me too. And God heard us," she murmured.

They didn't speak again until they were back at Steve's house. As he took the drowsy cat from her arms

204

and laid him on the sofa, he asked, "Will you stay and go with me tomorrow morning when I take Tommy?"

She reached up and touched his cheek. His skin felt smooth as a child's. "Of course I will, Steve."

He stood facing her, his hands lightly on her arms. "Oh, Andy!" he said, and the words seemed to erupt from some deep part of himself he rarely revealed. She felt his grip tighten; his chin puckered and his lower lip quivered as he fought for control. But the tears came anyway. His face reddened and he choked back sobs. Pulling her against him, he blurted, "Baby, I can't stand to lose anybody else!"

She stared up at him. "What do you mean, honey?"

"First my dad, when I was hardly twenty. He died in the spring, this same time of year. It was so sudden. And then you. Last year at this time I almost lost you. And now this year it's Tommy," he sobbed. "I just can't stand any more losses, Andy!"

"We'll pray for Tommy," she said soothingly, urging Steve over toward the sofa. "If God cares about a sparrow falling, He cares about Tommy." They sat and held Tommy between them and prayed for several minutes. Andy added her own silent prayer to their spoken words. *Oh, Lord, please help Steve get through this. He's so fragile and childlike in so many ways. For his sake, could You please heal this cat?*

How strange that since she had given Steve over to God and surrendered all claim to him, circumstances kept preventing her from telling him of her decision.

But there was something else to consider now too—a surprising new facet in the riddle of their relationship. These past few hours had given her a profound insight into this baffling man she had loved and puzzled over for so many months. He was almost like the man she had first fallen in love with—warm and tender, caring, vulnerable, and spontaneous. When had it all changed? Suddenly, she understood.

He changed when I got cancer last year. It was like he moved into his head; he knew how to help me and what to say to the doctors when I had surgery, but somehow, maybe because he was so scared, he distanced himself from me. And then he didn't know how to come back to me tenderly and lovingly, so he became analytical and intellectual about our relationship.

She remembered at the time telling him, "Someone else has taken over your body. You look the same, but you're not the same person." And he would reply with a note of irritation, "I don't know what you're talking about."

But now, seeing his reaction to Tommy, it was clear. Her cancer had frightened him. Clearly, he needed to be sure she wasn't going to die before he could allow himself to feel close to her again.

Did that mean she shouldn't break up with him after all? No, breaking up was inevitable after all the tensions between them this past year. Besides, Steve had given no sign that he was ready for a permanent relationship. They had been engaged nearly forever, but he seemed to consider engagement an end in itself, not a precursor to marriage. So she would wait for the opportune time to tell him he was free.

Early the next morning they drove Tommy back to the animal hospital and sat through the operation waiting and praying and sipping styrofoam cups of bitter coffee.

SHELTON & LANDIS

After what seemed like hours, the doctor emerged with a smile on his lips. "It's a miracle, Mr. Buckingham. We had to remove one kidney, but your cat lived through the surgery. Looks like he hasn't used up all nine of his lives yet. You can take him home tomorrow."

Steve smiled at Andy, his blue eyes dancing. "Are you free to come back with me tomorrow?"

"Don't worry," she said, hugging his arm. "I'm coming with you. We're seeing Tommy through this together!"

The next day, it was obvious Tommy was glad to be going home. With his bandages, he looked like a furry little war veteran, but his spirits were as high as ever. In the car, he purred loudly, licked Steve's hand in gratitude, and burrowed his nose into Andy's cascading hair.

That evening, after they had settled Tommy in for the night, Steve sat at the kitchen table reading the newspaper while Andy boiled some pasta for spaghetti. *Tonight I'll tell him,* she told herself. *Now that Tommy is okay, I'll tell him it's over between us.*

Unexpectedly Steve jumped up and strode over to her with the newspaper in hand. "Look, Andy."

She gazed at the paper. "What? I don't see—"

"They're advertising the Sara Lee Golf Tournament." His voice caught. "Every time I see those words, it reminds me—" He dropped the paper on the floor and drew her into his arms. "I could have lost you, Andy. I could have lost you!" He held her against him and buried his face in her hair. She could feel the wetness of his tears. "I'm sorry, Andy," he cried. "I'm so sorry I've withheld my love from you. I know you're doing the right thing by trying to help Bettye and Ricky. I'm sorry I haven't been more supportive of you."

"Oh, Steve—"

"I understand now, Andy," he rushed on earnestly. "Just like we prayed for Tommy, that's what you've been doing for Bettye and Ricky. I promise I'll try to help you more." He lifted her face to his. His eyes had never looked bluer. "Will you marry me, Andy?"

Had she heard right? *I'm just about to break up with this man, and he's proposing?* She stared open-mouthed at him. "You're confusing me, Steve."

He held her tighter, pressing her head against his chest, and gently brushed her tousled hair back from her face. "You're confused because I was confused, honey. But the thought of not having Tommy made me realize that it easily could have been *you*! I never want to lose you. Please, Andy, tell me you'll marry me!"

She drew back and gazed up at him. In that moment she knew that she loved him and would always love him, only him. With a coquettish little smile she murmured, "Get on your knees."

He looked puzzled. "On my knees? Andy, please don't make this harder for me than it has to be."

"I want to start over," she told him. "We've had some really bad months, and I don't want them to be part of our engagement. I want you to propose to me all over again."

With a gallant flourish he took her hand and got down on one knee beside her. He was wearing his gray sweats and a blue shirt that turned his eyes a deep cerulean blue. Irresistibly blue. "Andy, I've really been a fool," he said with exquisite tenderness, "and I'm so sorry. I love you. Will you marry me?"

She heard herself answer yes, and then he was on his feet enfolding her in his arms and kissing her lips; her head spun; she felt warm and small and protected in his arms.

Somewhere in her mind she was whispering a prayer; no, she was laughing and shouting a prayer. *God, You're amazing! This is truly a miracle! The cat gets sick, the cat gets better, and he asks me to marry him! How did You do that?*

CHAPTER 22

*E*arly in May, Ricky telephoned Bettye and said, "Just wanted to let you know I'm here in Cumming, Georgia, for a few days. I've got two nights of shows."

An impetuous idea struck Bettye. "Would you like me to come spend the weekend with you, Ricky? It's just a four-hour drive. I could leave in the morning and be there by noon."

"Sure, I'd like some company. Come on down."

The next morning, as she drove across the state line into Georgia, Bettye felt a keen sense of anticipation. She was keeping a rendezvous with her husband; it would be the first time in ages that they had been somewhere together outside the farmhouse. But she also felt as nervous as a cat on a telephone wire. What if these few days together strained their relationship even further? What if Ricky thought she was pushing too hard, expecting too much? *Dear God, please be with us! Help us to heal! Let this be the beginning of our reconciliation!*

She was wearing one of Ricky's favorite outfits—a silk peasant blouse that showed the curve of her shoulders, a full, clingy gauze skirt with tiny blue flowers against a

210

black and white background, and a wide black belt that accentuated her small waistline. Her loose auburn curls were pulled back from her face with tortoise shell combs, except for wispy tendrils that hung in spirals along her cheekbones. Black, old-fashioned laced ankle boots completed her outfit.

She arrived at the motel just before noon. Ricky's room was on the main floor—his usual preference—so that he could come and go unnoticed from the rear entrance. As she approached his room, her heart quickened. She was coming with high hopes but trying hard to have no expectations.

Moments after she rapped on his door, he appeared, his handsome, rangy frame filling the doorway. He was wearing a blue denim shirt and indigo blue jeans with his tan, pointed-toe, ostrich-skin boots. His shoulder-length, umber brown hair was combed back from his forehead revealing sun-bronzed skin with just the hint of a sheen. "Hi, Bettye. You're lookin' real good. How was your trip down?"

"It was fine, Ricky. I had the cool of the morning most of the way."

As they embraced, Bettye savored the smooth warmth of his cheek against hers and the natural masculine aroma of his skin. It had been so long since she had felt this close to him.

He released her and asked, "Are you hungry? I was thinking we could head over to Ryan's. I hear they've got the best wheat rolls in the South."

"Sure, I'd like that." Silently she marveled, *I can't remember the last time Ricky took me out to a restaurant!*

She glanced around the quaint little motel room

211

where a king-size bed claimed most of the space. Its brown chenille bedspread matched the simple chintz draperies and plain pine furnishings. It looked comfortable and pleasant, the sort of place where Ricky would feel at home. "Is it just us going to eat?" she asked.

"Yep. Just us."

Again she marveled. Usually Ricky never went out in public without his road manager, but today Bettye would have her husband all to herself!

Well, almost. As soon as they entered Ryan's buffet-style family restaurant, all heads turned their way. She kept her gaze focused straight ahead as people murmured and pointed.

"Can we have a table off in a corner somewhere?" Ricky asked the hostess, a nervous edge to his voice. She nodded and led them to a small table at the back of the restaurant.

When they were seated, Bettye said, "You stay here, Ricky. I'll go through the buffet line and get your food." She figured that would allow him some measure of privacy. Even before he was famous, Ricky hated being singled out or fussed over; he felt uncomfortable when people stared.

But even as she headed for the buffet table, Bettye noticed several people making their way toward Ricky. *Oh well,* she sighed. *It was almost just the two of us!*

She returned minutes later with a tray brimming with Ricky's favorites—turnip greens cooked in fatback, pinto beans, and macaroni and cheese, plus a leafy green salad for herself. Ricky was scrawling his signature on a paper napkin while a young boy waited in open-mouthed awe. Ricky handed him the autograph with a patient smile.

212

"Thanks, Mr. Shelton! You're the coolest!" The boy turned and dashed away, but Bettye heard him exclaim, "Look, Dad! I got Ricky Van Shelton's autograph!"

Bettye met Ricky's gaze with a smile of her own. "You may not get a chance to eat, you know. Maybe we should have ordered room service."

He gave her a sly wink. "And miss these homemade wheat rolls? Not on your life!"

Bettye reached across the table and touched his hand. "Ricky, I just want you to know, I really—"

"Excuse me, Mr. Shelton—aren't you Ricky Van Shelton?" A young couple in gray jogging suits stood gazing down at Ricky. The girl—a freckled strawberry blonde—shifted a chubby, tow-headed toddler in her arms and held out a torn piece of notebook paper. "We really hate to bother you while you're trying to eat, Mr. Shelton, but would you mind signing this for us?"

Ricky gave Bettye a knowing look and took the paper.

"Make it to Marty and Christina. And little Charlie." The girl shifted the child to the other hip. "I just love the song you sang with Dolly Parton, Mr. Shelton. Just ask Marty. I play it all the time."

The wiry, sandy-haired man nodded vigorously. "She does. She plays it all the time!"

"Thank you," said Ricky, handing back the paper.

He lifted a forkful of greens to his lips, but an elderly couple in their Sunday best were already approaching, pen and paper in hand. The woman leaned down conspiratorially. "We *hate* bothering you while you're eating, but would you mind—?"

Bettye thought wearily, *You don't hate it as much as me!*

"Sure," Ricky replied, taking the pen the woman offered.

"We've got front row seats for your concert tonight," said the man. "We're bringing the whole family—my brother Ned and his wife, and Martha's cousin Greta and her three kids, and—"

Ricky's smile remained in place, but Bettye noticed him tweaking the tip of his collar with his thumb. *He can't wait to get out of here,* she noted solemnly.

"He don't wanna hear all that, Frank," said the woman. "Look, the poor man's trying to eat!"

Ricky signed the paper and gave it back to her. In his melodious Virginian accent, he said, "Enjoy the show tonight, folks."

Bettye sighed with relief when she and Ricky returned to his motel room an hour later. At last some privacy! "I'm hardly ever out in public with you," she told him. "I forget what it's like dealing with all that attention."

"Sometimes it's real hard," he agreed. "But they're my fans, Bettye. Where would I be without them?" He faced her and ran his hand lightly over her shoulder along the gathered neckline of her blouse. "Listen, Bettye, I gotta go do the sound check for tonight's show. I'll be back soon, okay?"

She quelled her disappointment. "Sure, Ricky. I'll be here. I'm not going anywhere." *Maybe we can still find a few minutes to spend together before the concert.*

But when Ricky returned from the sound check, he collapsed onto the bed and murmured, "I gotta catch a couple hours of shut-eye before the show."

Bettye understood. It was important for Ricky to be well rested before he performed. His concerts demanded every ounce of his energy; he had to be at his best. But would there ever be time for the two of them alone, or had Bettye made this trip to Georgia in vain?

That night, by the time the concert was over and Ricky had sung several encores and met with fans holding backstage passes, it was well after midnight. He and Bettye returned to their room exhausted, shed their clothes, and fell into bed with hardly a word between them. Within minutes, Ricky was asleep, the rhythm of his breathing deep and steady and wonderfully familiar. Bettye drifted into slumber too, savoring the physical warmth of her husband beside her in bed for the first time in months.

They slept late the next morning, waking to warm sunshine and delicious silence, except for the twittering birdsong outside their window. Bettye stretched contentedly between smooth sheets, relishing Ricky's closeness. This was the way it was meant to be!

They rose shortly after nine. Ricky called room service and ordered coffee and bagels for breakfast.

After they had eaten, Bettye gave Ricky a vigorous back massage for nearly an hour; his muscles were always so tight and tense after a show. Then, as a few guarded kisses gave way to ardor and yearning, they came together as husband and wife and made love for the first time in a long while, and this time Bettye knew there was truth and honesty between them.

Ricky made no promises. He didn't tell her he loved her. But the deep feelings were still there. They both knew the embers of desire could be kindled again into flames of passion. It was a profound step toward healing their relationship.

Afterward, as Bettye lay in his arms, Ricky said huskily, "I think you should give up the townhouse and come home. I don't know what's ahead for us, but we can find out better if you're back livin' at the farm."

SHELTON & LANDIS

*O*n May 13, 1991, Bettye packed her things and moved out of the townhouse in Nashville. Without regret she left the place she had called her sanctuary. It had served its purpose; in its walls she had found solace and comfort through her friendships with Andy and Linda. Through countless prayer sessions the three of them had tapped into and claimed the power of the Holy Spirit in their lives. Bettye was leaving this phase of her life a stronger, more centered and confident person.

She had known all along that her townhouse was only a temporary abode; she had never hung a picture or set out her own knickknacks or even purchased curios or gadgets for this home away from home. She left it as neutral and untouched and anonymous as she had found it.

But Bettye had no intention of giving up the friendships she had nurtured at the townhouse. She promptly telephoned Andy and Linda to let them know they could reach her now at the farm.

"We have so much to catch up on," Andy told her when she called. "Let's get together soon. I want to hear

217

what's happening with you and I'll tell you the latest about Steve and me."

"I have an idea," said Bettye. "I'm going to the TNN/Music City News Awards Show in June and I really want to look like a knock-out for Ricky. But I've never known how to put clothes together. You've been a model, Andy. Will you come help me pick out the right dress?"

"Girl, I'll help you pick out a wardrobe that'll knock Ricky's socks off."

"Terrific! Where shall we go? Nashville?"

"How about Atlanta? They have great clothes."

"All right. My sister lives in Atlanta. Maybe she could join us for a real shopping spree."

On May 24th, Bettye and Andy drove to Atlanta and picked up Bettye's sister, Linda East. That evening the three of them checked into a luxury suite at Lennox Square, a lush hotel on Peachtree Street. The suite had a lovely living room, kitchen, dining area, two bathrooms, and a large master bedroom that Bettye and Linda would share. Andy would take the couch in the living room that made up into a bed.

"This is the life," said Andy as they walked from room to room, marveling. "It's beautiful! Look at the plush carpet and drapes."

"And the velvet wallpaper," said Linda.

"It's like a fantasy, isn't it?" said Bettye. "And re-member, we can pamper ourselves as much as we please. Ricky said he'll pick up the tab."

"Just like that—he agreed?"

"I told him I really needed this—a girls' weekend away to shop and have fun with Andy and my sister."

"Tell him thanks," said Linda, "for all of us."

"Hey, girls," called Andy, "I've got room service on the phone. What do you want for dinner?"

"Something delicious, elegant, expensive, and fattening," said Linda, prompting their laughter.

As they ate Caesar salads, lobster, prime rib, and angel hair pasta at the large cherry wood dining table, they gazed out the window at the galaxy of city lights speckling the darkness. "I could get used to living like this," said Andy. "First thing in the morning I'm going to the health spa downstairs and getting a massage."

"Me, too," said Linda, "after I've had breakfast in bed!"

"We'll select whatever we please," said Bettye. "We're not scrimping on anything."

And they didn't. In the morning they ordered fresh fruit, juice, croissants, and delicious chamomile tea with honey. They ate at a leisurely pace, sipping their tea slowly from delicate china cups, feeling every inch like royalty. Their suite was cozy and pleasant; sunlight streamed through the window, casting a burnished glow on the walls and furniture.

"Nothing can make me budge from this spot," said Andy, stretching out her long legs on the brocade sofa and tossing back her thick mane of hair.

"Does the word *shopping* mean anything to you?" asked Linda with a wry smile.

Andy sat at attention. "Shopping? As in shopping spree?"

"Before we go shopping, I have a little gift for each of you," said Bettye, handing each of them an envelope. "I don't want this to be just *my* shopping trip. I want you

219

SHE STAYS

both to take this money and splurge on something you really want."

"Bettye, you don't have to do this," protested Andy.

"I want to. It makes me happy."

"Okay." Andy broke into a grin and her luminous green eyes danced. "Then I say it's time we head for the mall!"

One of the first shops they visited that morning was a shoe store, where Andy found a pair of black patent leather flats. "I have such long, skinny feet," she lamented as she slipped her foot into one shoe, "but look, these fit! And they have pennies and buttons on top. When I was a kid, I thought my guardian angel's name was Penny. I used to say, 'Penny, are you with me?' These shoes will remind me of my angel. I've got to have them!"

After Andy got her shoes, they walked a few doors down to an exclusive women's shop where Bettye tried on several dresses for the upcoming awards show. Andy, Linda, and even the saleslady uttered exclamations of approval when Bettye stepped out in a fitted, white brocade dress with a heart-shaped bodice and spaghetti straps. Covering the dress was a sheer coat with brocade around the cuffs and down the front.

"Now that is a sexy dress!" declared Andy. "You look incredible, Bettye, especially with your golden tan and great figure!"

"It's stunning," Linda agreed. "It fits you like a glove."

Bettye's face flushed with warmth and excitement. "This is the dress I want," she agreed as she examined her

220

reflection in the surrounding mirrors. "Those twenty-year-old girls don't have anything on me!"

"It's a bit long," said the saleslady. "You'll want it just above the knee. Don't worry, we'll take care of the alterations. If you'll stand on this little pedestal, I'll mark the hem."

Bettye stepped up on the pedestal and stood motionless while the woman made the necessary measurements. The room was growing warm, too warm; a sweat broke out on Bettye's skin. Her legs felt weak. She tried to focus her eyes on Andy and Linda, but her vision blurred. She could hear them talking and laughing, but the sounds seemed to be coming at her from a distance. "It's so hot," she complained, but the saleslady was too absorbed in making her chalk marks to notice. Bettye felt a wave of nausea roll through her stomach. She swayed. "I think I better sit down."

Andy and Linda rushed to her side, their voices full of concern as they offered a steadying hand. "Are you all right?" asked Andy, taking her arm.

They led her over to a chair. "Tell us what's wrong!" urged Linda. "Your face is white as a sheet."

"I think I'm going to pass out," Bettye murmured. A sudden, horrendous pain streaked through her lower back. It stole her breath and left her faint with pain. She cried out as her legs buckled under her.

Andy and Linda caught her and eased her down gently on the chair. Her head spun; her back was in agony. The saleslady ran out and returned a minute later with a paper cup of lukewarm water. "What can we do for you, dear? Shall I call an ambulance?"

"No," Bettye managed, "I just need to lie down."

S H E   S T A Y S

"Our hotel is close by," said Andy. "We'll help her back to her room."

Somehow they made their way back to Lennox Square, but, for Bettye, the next few hours passed as fleeting blips of memory with large blank spaces between. Gripped by excruciating pain, she was vaguely aware of Linda helping her into bed; a local doctor came in, examined her, and asked countless medical questions, none of which anchored themselves in her spinning brain. He said something about her kidneys and told her to see her regular doctor for a thorough exam. And he gave her antibiotics and pain pills that knocked her out for the rest of the night.

The next day Andy dropped Linda off at her house, then drove Bettye home. They were all keenly disappointed that their shopping trip had ended so abruptly. At least Bettye's pain was subsiding, and she was feeling better. When she saw her doctor later that day, he told her she was probably suffering from a kidney infection and to continue taking the antibiotics.

Assuming the kidney attack was an isolated incident, Bettye tried to put the painful memory behind her; she wanted to look forward now to the TNN/Music City News Award Show coming on June 10th. And when her white brocade dress arrived from the Atlanta store, she knew she had just the right outfit for that special night.

Bettye's two brothers and their wives—Chester and Brenda Witt and Ricky and Pam Witt—came to attend the awards show with Bettye and Ricky. They all rode into Nashville in Ricky's tour bus, and all the way Bettye felt like a princess in her stunning white brocade dress.

That evening, as they took their seats in the Grand

Ole Opry theater, the atmosphere was charged with excitement. The amphitheater-style auditorium held two tiers containing a total of forty-four hundred seats; all seats faced the stage, which contained a circle of flooring from the original Ryman Auditorium stage where the greatest country singers of all time had performed—Roy Acuff, Hank Williams, and Patsy Cline. The curtains across the front of the stage were several stories high.

The brightest and the best performers in the country music industry milled about as television cameras jockeyed for position, producers gave last minute instructions, and musicians tuned their instruments. Bettye watched the influx of people taking their seats. Women wore designer gowns, silk dresses, and expensive jewelry. The men wore black tuxedos with ten gallon Stetsons and hand-painted boots.

Then, suddenly, everything fell into place; the music swelled, the cameras rolled, and the award presentations began. Before long, Bettye heard Ricky's name announced. "And for Male Vocalist of the Year, the fans have spoken. It's Ricky Van Shelton!"

Ricky gave her a quick hug before he made his way up to the stage. She watched with love and pride as he accepted the award. This awards show was more important to him than any other, because it was the fans who were voting, not industry insiders. Before the program was over, Ricky's name was called again. "Voted by the fans as the Entertainer of the Year for 1991 is . . . Ricky Van Shelton!"

Bettye clapped with delight as Ricky got up, looking dazed with amazement, and headed for the stage a second time. He had just won the two most coveted awards a

_223_

singer could receive. Over the past few years he had won many awards—four, in fact, at last year's TNN/Music City News Award Show—but until now he had never won Entertainer of the Year.

When Ricky took his seat again, he whispered to her, "I can't believe they gave this to me. There's Reba McEntire, George Strait—they're entertainers; I'm a singer, not an entertainer."

"The fans think you're a great entertainer, Ricky," she assured him. "You can't argue with the fans."

After the show, Ricky and Bettye, her brothers and their wives returned to his tour bus. A steady flow of industry people came by to congratulate Ricky; they shook his hand, slapped him on the back, and told him how happy they were for him. Ricky was jubilant, but already he was reaching for a drink; Bettye knew it would be the first of many this evening, as usual. The buzz of conversation and laughter began to whirl in her mind. She sat down and immediately felt the same vivid streak of pain across her back.

It's this dress! She stiffened and forced herself to remain calm. *Just sit still,* she told herself. *Smile and pretend everything's okay. Don't spoil Ricky's special evening.*

Bettye managed to keep her backache a secret until she arrived home late that night. As she crawled into bed, she realized the pain was subsiding. Maybe she would be all right after all. No sense in complaining to Ricky. He had only a few hours to sleep before he had to rise at dawn and drive back into Nashville for Fan Fair Week—a momentous, annual country music event. Every June thousands upon thousands of eager fans came to the Nashville fairgrounds to meet their favorite artists, get their autographs, and have their pictures taken with them. Ricky would be meeting fans at his booth from early morning until late at night.

With all he's got on his mind, he doesn't need to be worrying about me, she decided as he turned out the light and climbed into bed beside her. "Get some shut-eye, Ricky," she told him. "It's been a big, wonderful day, and it'll be another big day tomorrow." *And, Lord willing, my back will be fine in the morning and you'll never have to know how badly I was hurting.*

Ricky was already gone the next morning when Bettye got up and began fixing breakfast for her brothers and their wives before they headed back to Virginia. Her back was better, but the pain lingered, so she moved cautiously around the kitchen as she put on coffee and placed bread in the toaster.

"Are you okay, Bettye?" Chester asked as he helped himself to the coffee. "You're moving around here real slow."

"Oh, I just have a little backache, that's all."

"Well, you had better be careful. Don't overdo it. You go back to bed when we leave."

"Sure, I'll do that, but I'm just fine."

She managed to keep quiet about her lower back pain until her family was safely out the door. After all, no sense in worrying them; they would just delay their trip, and they had a long drive ahead of them. But as soon as their automobile disappeared down the road, she went back upstairs and lay down on the bed.

All morning she had managed to dismiss her pain, but she could no longer deny its severity. Over the next hour the racking spasms became so harrowing she almost screamed out in torment.

She reached for the phone and called the physician who had treated her after her return from Atlanta. "I'm in terrible pain," she told him. "I don't know what to do."

"Bettye, you need to come to the hospital right away."

"I—I can't get out of bed."

"Do you want me to send an ambulance?"

"No, I don't want an ambulance. I'll call my husband."

"All right, but just get to the hospital as soon as possible. My office is across the street. They'll call me when you arrive. Come straight to the emergency room."

When she had hung up, Bettye lay back and sighed. She had told the doctor, *I'll call my husband.* Easier said than done. How could she reach Ricky at Fan Fair? She picked up the phone again and dialed Ricky's manager. "I've got to talk to Ricky."

"What's wrong, Bettye?"

"I'm in terrible pain. I've got to go to the hospital, and I want to talk to my husband."

"Do you want us to give him the message and tell him to come out?"

"No! I want to talk to my husband." She was crying now. "I want my husband!"

"Bettye, he'll be right there!"

She hung up the receiver and put her head back on the pillow and wept. With the traffic and crowds at Fan Fair, it would take Ricky nearly two hours to get home. Could she wait that long?

SHELTON & LANDIS

But forty minutes later she heard Ricky's car barreling up the driveway. The car door slammed, then she heard him running up the stairs. He burst into the room, his face damp with sweat, his hair flying around his collar. He sank down on his knees next to the bed and clasped her hand. She had never seen such fear and concern in his eyes. "What is it, Bettye? What's wrong?"

Tears of relief flowed now. "I can't move," she told him. "It hurts so bad. It's my back."

"What can I do?"

"The doctor is waiting for me at the hospital."

"Then let's go." He wrapped his arms around her and helped her off the bed. "Put your weight on me, Bettye." He carefully maneuvered her down the stairs, out the door, and into the car. "Don't worry, baby. I'll have you there before you know it. Whatever this is, we'll fight it together."

When they arrived at the hospital, Ricky checked her in and made sure she was settled comfortably in her room. He sat by her bed as they waited for the doctor. "Ricky, what about Fan Fair?" she asked. "Everyone must be wondering where you are."

"I called while you were getting settled in. I canceled the rest of the day. I'm staying here, Bettye, until we know what's wrong."

"But you have Fan Fair all week and you're back on the road after that. You can't cancel your concerts."

"I'm staying here until the doctor says you're okay. And when you get out of the hospital, I'll have your folks come stay with you while I'm away."

Bettye stayed in the hospital for three days, receiving intravenous antibiotics while doctors ran a battery of tests. Their diagnosis? Severe kidney infection. Her doctor speculated that it could have been caused by bacteria or something else. "Anybody can get such an infection at any time," he explained. "Chances are it will never happen again."

But Bettye already knew what she would remember most from this distressing incident: In a crisis her husband would be there for her.

In June, 1991, just as Bettye and Ricky were rekindling the intimacy between them, Ricky began his heavy tour season. Out of the one hundred and fifty to two hundred concerts he performed each year, many were county fair dates scheduled for the summer months. He would be on the road for weeks at a time, then home for a few days before hitting the road again. It was no way to revive a struggling marriage.

Although he and Bettye were living together again as husband and wife, he made no promises about their future. "I need time. I'm still not sure what I want," he told her over and over. "A lot's happened between the two of us and it's gonna take time for me to know what's gonna be." He went on to assure her there would be no other women as long as they were together.

But Ricky was still drinking heavily and getting drunk night after night. The next morning he would get up and say, "That's it. Never again. I'll never drink again. I'm gonna give this stuff up!"

Bettye made a point not to pressure him about his drinking. Every time she felt the urge to tell him what he should or shouldn't do, the Holy Spirit reminded her that

228

it was her job to *love* Ricky, and it was God's job to *fix* him.

"I can stay sober," Ricky promised again and again. "This is the last time I get drunk!"

But, of course, it wasn't.

Several times he called Bettye from the road and said, "I haven't had a beer. I didn't drink a single beer last night!" Her hopes soared until she found out he had given up beer for wine. He was getting drunk every night on wine!

Sometimes when he was home he would tell her, "I've been praying to quit drinking. I've been trying." At other times he would say with a sigh of resignation, "I asked the Lord to help me stop drinking, but He doesn't hear my prayers." Finally he admitted, "The Lord just isn't there for me anymore."

Ricky spent the weekend of July 20th at the farm filming the video, "Keep It Between the Lines," a simple, heart-tugging song that stressed eternal truths, family ties, and basic values. Bettye was grateful for the song's message. She felt God had brought it into Ricky's life to remind him of the importance of loving one's family, trusting God, and doing what was right. Now if only he would get the message!

*I*n the fall of 1991, Bettye started back to school and immersed herself in her studies. With Ricky gone more than he was at home, their marriage remained on hold. His West Coast tour kept him on the road for the entire month of November performing both in Canada and the United States, including Washington, Oregon, Nevada, Idaho, Utah, Montana, North Dakota, and California.

Bettye worried about him being away from home for so many weeks at a time. Ricky often claimed that it was the boredom of traveling constantly on his bus that drove him to drink. "There's nothing else to do out there," he would lament.

Every day Bettye prayed, "Dear Lord, be with him; bear him up; help him to stop drinking." And then he'd call her the next morning hung over and moan, "I keep praying for the Lord to stop this drinking, but the Lord won't hear me!"

And then one morning it all came to a riveting head. At 5:30 A.M. on November 25th, Bettye's phone rang. Groggily she reached for the receiver, put it to her ear, and murmured, "Hello?"

The voice on the other end sounded garbled, out of control. It was Ricky. He was sobbing, riding the edge of hysteria. "Ricky, what's wrong?" she cried.

The words tumbled out between sobs, wrenching, incomprehensible. "God stole my gun, Bettye. God stole my gun!"

"Ricky, what are you talking about?"

"I gotta come home, Bettye. Can I come home?"

She was wide awake now, her heart racing. "Yes, Ricky, you can come home. What's wrong?"

He wrung out the words with a mournful torment. "I —I can't stand it anymore. They want everything they can get from me, and it's too late. I've sold my soul. I've sold my soul to the devil, and now they even want the money he paid me for my soul!"

Bettye's fingers cramped as she squeezed the receiver. Barbs of panic prickled her spine. "Ricky, you're out of your head. What's wrong? Where are you?"

"I'm in Los Angeles. On my bus. I've got a seven A.M. call to tape a TV show, but I can't do it, Bettye." His voice throbbed with despair. "I just . . . I just gotta come home. I wanna be home, Bettye. Don't tell anyone. Don't even tell them I called you."

"Ricky, please—tell me what happened?"

"Don't let them know, Bettye," he insisted. "They'll come after me. They'll make me come back. Don't tell them."

"Ricky, I won't tell anybody." She was out of bed now, pacing the floor, twisting the coiled phone cord around her fingers. "How are you coming home?"

"My driver, Murf. I called him at the hotel. And my backup driver."

"Is Murf there now?"

"No. Nobody's here. I'm all alone."

"What about your road manager, your band, the crew?"

"They're all at the hotel." He choked out the words. "I'm all alone and the gun's gone. My gun's gone, Bettye."

Her mouth went dry. "What gun, Ricky?"

"The gun. *My* gun. The thirty-eight pistol I got hid in a secret place by my bed. It's gone. God stole it!"

Bettye sat down on the edge of her bed, her legs weak, unsteady. "What do you mean, God stole it?"

"God stole it. The gun is gone and I was looking for it. It's not where I hid it."

She forced the words out over the sandpaper taste in her mouth. "What do you want the gun for, Ricky?"

"I needed the gun. I had to have the gun. I wanted it."

An icy fist squeezed her heart. "Why, Ricky?"

She could hear his voice suddenly breaking into great, heaving sobs. "I . . . I wanted to kill myself!"

"Oh, Ricky, no!" Tears stung her own eyes and streamed down her cheeks. She gripped the receiver as if it were a lifeline. Her fingers ached. She had never felt so helpless and scared. How many thousands of miles stretched between Nashville and California? It might as well have been the other side of the world. "Ricky," she cried, "are you still there?"

"I'm here, Bettye."

"Is Murf there yet?"

"No, not yet."

"Tell me when Murf comes. Ricky, don't hang up on me!"

"I don't wanna hang up. I wanna come home."

"Just keep talking to me, Ricky." Her heart was pounding like a hammer; surely he could hear. "Everything is okay now," she said as if comforting a child. "You're going to come home. Everything's fine. Just wait till Murf gets there. Just keep talking to me until Murf gets there."

"Where is Murf?" said Ricky, sounding peeved. "Why isn't he here? I can't stand it anymore."

Bettye rocked back and forth on the bed, feeling the icy chill in her chest crawl through her limbs. "I know, Ricky. I know. You just hang on, baby, okay?"

"Bettye, I love you." He sounded like a little boy, needy, lost, alone.

Keep it steady, calm, she told herself. "I love you too, Ricky."

He was still weeping. "I want to come home."

It broke her heart. "I want you to come home too, Ricky," she said over the lump in her throat. "You're coming home. You'll be home soon. Murf will be there in just a minute. He's coming. I know he's coming."

There was silence for a moment, then over the phone she heard Murf entering the bus and saying, "What's wrong, boss?" Ricky said, "Murf, take me home," and he replied, "Okay, man, we're going home."

She could hear rustling sounds—Murf getting things ready to go. She could imagine Murf—a big, quiet, gentle man in his mid-twenties—putting his night bag up and checking things on the bus. Then she heard the roar of the engine.

233

SHE STAYS

Ricky came back on the phone and said, "Murf's here. Bettye, I'm coming home."

"Ricky, you're all right now," she said soothingly.

"I'm so tired," he sighed. "So tired!"

"Baby, it's okay. I'm here. I'm waiting. Ricky, do you think you can sleep?"

"Yeah, I'm tired." His voice was heavy now, the words coming more slowly. "I just can't take it no more. I gotta come home. Don't tell nobody."

"I won't, Ricky. I promise."

"They're all waiting. I'm supposed to be there in the morning, and I'm not gonna be there, and they'll look for me. They'll have people trying to bring me back. But I can't. I've got to get away."

"I know, Ricky. It's okay."

He was sounding calmer. "I'm hanging up now, Bettye. I gotta go lay down."

"Okay, Ricky. You call me when you get up. Just call me. I need to hear from you again."

"I will." His voice took on unexpected tenderness. "Bettye, I love you so much. I don't want to lose you!"

"You're not losing me, Ricky." Her tears started again. "I'm here for you. I'm here."

She hung up the phone and sat still for a long while, hardly daring to breathe. Her body felt stiff, frozen in a gesture of alarm. Tension had locked her muscles tight; she ached from the back of her neck to the joints of her toes. With painful effort she moved, arching her shoulders, shifting her torso, stretching her toes. As the first fragile rays of dawn broke through the darkness, she whispered, "Dear God, help Ricky now. Bring him home safe. Please get him home."

234

She paced her room with an urgent, nervous energy. What now? She had to do something. She had prayed, but she needed more prayers. Of course—Andy! She seized the phone. Her fingers trembled as she dialed.

After several rings, Andy said hello, her voice thick with sleep.

"Andy, it's Bettye. Something's happened with Ricky."

Andy was suddenly alert. "What's wrong?"

"I don't know. Ricky's on his way home. It's major. I'm scared, Andy. He was talking out of his head. He's desperate. It had something to do with a gun."

Andy expelled a sharp breath. "Oh, Bettye!"

"I don't know what to do, Andy."

"I know you're scared, Bettye, but we've prayed for Ricky to come back to God," said Andy with calm resolve. "This is it. He's hit bottom, and now he's going to have to choose. Let's pray right now for God to protect Ricky and bring him back to Him."

After they had prayed, Bettye sighed audibly and said, "I feel better, Andy. You're right. We have to stand firm."

"Remember, Bettye, you're not alone. God's here. The angels are here. I'm here. I'll be praying for you and Ricky."

"Ricky's got Murf with him, too; Murf will take care of him," said Bettye. "If anybody asks you, Andy, don't say anything about where Ricky is or what's going on."

"Don't worry, Bettye. I won't tell anyone. Not even Steve."

"Thanks, Andy. I can't tell you how much your prayers and friendship mean to me."

Shortly after Bettye hung up the phone, Ricky's management on the West Coast called, sounding urgent. "Bettye, have you heard from Ricky?"

"Yes, I have."

"Where is he?"

"I don't know. Something happened. He's had enough."

"Well, nothing was wrong last night when we left him. He was on the bus and everything was fine; no problem. He's got a show to do, Bettye."

"Leave him alone," she said staunchly. "Just let go of him. He's coming home!"

———◆———

"Andy, where's Ricky?"

Steve was on the phone, his voice edged with fury and desperation.

Andy's neck muscles tightened. She licked her lips. "I don't know, Steve." It had been only hours since Bettye's urgent call asking for prayer for Ricky, and Andy could still hear Bettye's solemn warning, *Don't tell anyone!*

"I know you know where he is," Steve persisted, his tone ominous. "Tell me, Andy. Where is Ricky?" In the background she could hear the commotion in Steve's office—doors slamming and several people talking at once, their voices shrill and irate.

Oh, no! The pressure is on over this! "I can't, Steve," she blurted. "I don't know. I can't talk about it."

"Have you heard from Bettye?"

"Yes, I did hear from her this morning."

"Does she know where he is?"

"I—I can't tell you."

"Listen, Andy, people are frantic around here. The

network's been calling, wanting to know, 'Where's Ricky Van Shelton?' He never showed up for his seven A.M. call. The band woke up and he was gone; no note, no phone call, nothing. The bus is gone. We don't know whether he went off on a drunken binge with some woman, or if he's gone off to kill himself, or what. They've even got the state troopers out looking for him. If you know anything about this, Andy, you'd better tell me."

"I don't know where he is, Steve. You're going to have to trust me. It'll be okay."

His voice deepened, taking on a rough emotional edge. "Yeah, well, I don't know how this can turn out okay. Okay for who? His managers are calling; everybody's calling. This is serious, Andy."

Her stomach knotted. "I don't know what to tell you, honey, but I just know Ricky's going to be all right. This is what we've been praying for."

"You do know something." He sounded wounded, betrayed. "But you're not going to tell me what you know, are you?"

"I can't, Steve. I really don't know anything."

"Yeah, sure. I'll just tell people, 'Sorry, Andy doesn't know where Ricky is.'"

"Can't you just tell them he's sick and can't perform?"

Steve's tone hardened. "Don't worry about it, Andy. It's not your problem."

The line went dead, and Andy sat back, stunned. What had she just done? Once again she had been loyal to Bettye only to hurt the man she loved. Steve had never sounded so betrayed.

She twisted the engagement ring Steve had put back

237

on her finger last Easter. She thought about that Sunday when they found the land where they were presently building their dream house—rolling hills with grazing cattle and a creek running through vivid green grasses. They had stood together on the top of that hill, with the wind blowing in their faces and billowing clouds almost so close they could touch them, and they had looked at each other and said, "This is it!" This was where they wanted to spend the rest of their lives.

Now that magnificent house was almost complete, but would she ever share it with Steve? Had their bond of love and trust snapped with a single phone call? That's how it felt. Steve would forever question her loyalty; he would always be convinced she put others first. Perhaps he would even change his mind about marrying her. After all, what kind of wife put everyone else before her husband?

Darkness settled over Andy's spirits. She imagined herself losing her land and her home and the man she cherished. Everything dear to her was spinning out away from her, beyond her grasp.

"Dear God, why do You keep putting me in this tug of war between two people I care so much about? You're asking me to sacrifice too much, Lord—my chance to have a happy, healthy relationship with the man I love."

———— • ◦ • ————

Ricky didn't call Bettye again until Tuesday morning, a day later. As soon as she heard his voice on the phone, her pulse quickened. "Ricky, are you okay?"

"I'm all right, Bettye." He was speaking calmly, clearly.

"What happened?" she cried. "What's going on with you?"

"I've been in the back of my bus now for twenty-four hours. I've been crying out to God. I've been praying and I've been crying." He paused and his voice grew somber. "Bettye, I saw the devil back there in my bus."

Bettye's heart lurched. "What, Ricky? What are you saying?"

"He came to kill me, Bettye. I saw him. I was lying in my bed as we were traveling down the highway. I was miserable, crying out to God to help me quit drinking. And I saw the devil standing over me, big as life. He was in my face, sneering at me. It was horrible, Bettye. I could feel the heat of his breath and smell the stench. I couldn't breathe because he was right up in my face, and he was laughing at me."

"Ricky, what did you do?"

"I tried to hit him. I started swinging my arms, boxing like Muhammad Ali. I hit him over and over and over again, and he didn't move. I laid back on my bed gasping for breath and my heart was pounding like a jackhammer. I thought, I'm gonna get my wish; I'm gonna die! Tears were streaming down my face, but the devil just kept laughing. It was like he was telling me he had me. But do you know what I did, Bettye?"

"What, Ricky?"

"I was swinging at him and he didn't budge. So finally I looked at him and I said, 'I might not be able to beat you, but I know somebody who can. God can beat you; Jesus can!' And, you know, Bettye, the devil's eyes got round as quarters and he drew back like he'd been struck hard; and he just disappeared. Vanished, just like that! I couldn't do it myself, Bettye, but God got rid of him!"

"That's wonderful, Ricky. I'm so glad." She wanted to jump up and shout, *Hallelujah!* How often had the words, *I can do it myself,* rung in her memory? Ricky had constantly told her he had to do it himself, whether it was giving up alcohol or other women or making his marriage work; he insisted on doing it alone, his way, without anyone else's help. Now, for the first time he was admitting he couldn't do it himself; he needed God's help!

"Bettye—" A pang of regret shaded his voice. "Bettye, I got drunk again last night. There were women on the bus, and I was so drunk I couldn't hardly even see them. We were partying and then it was just me and one woman by ourselves. I didn't do anything, Bettye, but I would've. I know I would've, except God sobered me up, and I saw what I was doing. I saw her sitting there waiting, and I knew I was about to do it again. I knew I was a failure and I knew I couldn't keep my promise to you, so I sent her away and I went to get my gun. I wanted to die last night, Bettye. I wanted to blow my brains out."

"Ricky," she said, her guard up suddenly, "what gun are you talking about?"

"My gun. I had a thirty-eight pistol in my bus, back in a hidden compartment beside my bed. I've had it there for months, and nobody knows it's back there, not even Murf. Nobody would even know how to find that compartment. Only me. And nobody comes in my room anyway; I have all my stuff in there, and nobody bothers my stuff."

"I know, Ricky. Tell me about the gun."

"I went to get it because I was gonna kill myself, and

240

the gun was gone. I know now God stole my gun. God took it because He knew what I was gonna do. He saved my life, Bettye."

She gripped the receiver. She was already praying—praising God, entreating Him for her husband. "Just come on home now, okay, Ricky? Just come on home."

"I'll be there sometime in the middle of the night. I'll be there, Bettye."

"And I'll be waiting for you, darling."

As soon as she hung up, she phoned Andy. "I just talked to Ricky," she said, her voice prickling with excitement. After relating Ricky's account of his experience on the bus, she concluded, "This is a major turning point, Andy. Yesterday I thought it was a breakdown. But today I know it's a break *through*."

"Bettye, Ricky is going to be fine by Christmas."

"What?" Andy's words came out of the blue.

"Ricky will be fine by Christmas," she repeated with conviction.

"Yeah, Andy, I think so, too. He's going to be fine by Christmas."

CHAPTER 25

*B*ettye waited up for Ricky into the early hours of the morning. She paced the floor, listening for the rumble of his bus in the driveway; the living room lights were on low and the house was eerily silent. The hands of the clock seemed to be moving in slow motion. She sat down in Ricky's brown high-backed La-Z-Boy and ran her hands over the cushioned arms as she recalled the good times with her husband.

She remembered the times they drove on country back roads for hours listening to Willie Nelson and David Allen Coe on the radio, and the times they frolicked outdoors like children chasing and squirting each other with a garden hose. She recalled the sweet little yellow house they bought before they built this home. They loved that little country house. Ricky's career was just starting to take off. At any hour of the day or night she would drive him to the service station right off the interstate to meet his tour bus. Those were precious, exciting days.

Bettye stood up and walked some more, wearing off the nervous energy of anticipation. She was too keyed up to relax. What would Ricky be like when he got home? Agitated? Depressed?

She ran her hand over a small bench Ricky had made years ago—a slab of maple he had cut down the center lengthwise. He had sanded the surface to a smooth buttery grain. The bottom was still rounded like the log and the legs were cut from smaller logs.

Behind the sofa stood a larger bench Ricky had made of lumber cut from river maples that grew on the farm. The bench was covered with Bettye's plants, but under it stood a collection of Ricky's childhood toys, including a football from elementary school and a 1950s metal two-story garage with small painted cars. Looking at the toys he loved reminded her of the little boy in Ricky—his bashfulness, his sincerity, his genteel manners, his mischievousness.

But there was so much more to the simple, homespun man she loved. She gazed at the wall where his oil paintings, watercolors, and pastel drawings hung. The renderings captured Ricky's favorite places back home in Virginia—the Blue Ridge Mountains, old log buildings in the meadows near his parents' home, and a country church in a little village blanketed with snow and glistening in the moonlight.

"Dear Lord, please let my husband be the man he used to be," she prayed.

It was nearly two in the morning when Bettye heard Ricky's bus grind to a halt in the driveway. Her sense of expectancy had mushroomed in the past few hours; she was keenly alert, every muscle taut. She waited until she heard Ricky's boots on the porch before throwing open the door to him. He stood in the doorway looking like a soldier returned from battle—jacket rumpled, hair wind-blown, shoulders sagging, chin riding his chest. She stared into his face and saw something she had never seen before—the look of a man who had experienced things he could never put into words; a survivor's shell-shocked gaze glinted in his suede-green eyes.

She went into his arms and they held each other for a long time. Neither of them spoke; words were unnecessary. She had never loved him so much, nor felt such love and neediness from him. They broke their embrace only to hug again, and again, both desperately hungry for the other's closeness and warmth.

Finally they released each other and he lumbered into the room like a traveler who had walked too many miles with a heavy load. He sank down in his chair and closed his eyes. "I'm so tired," he said. "So plumb tired!"

———◆———

The weeks that followed were quiet ones at the farm-house. Bettye could see how troubled her husband was, but she didn't push him to talk. They spent nights sitting close on the couch holding hands and watching television. She would massage his back and shoulders or sit at the end of the couch and rub his feet. She gave Ricky all her attention, all her love.

His management canceled the rest of his tour dates for the year, except for a couple of engagements in mid-December, acknowledging that he had been under too much strain. Everyone agreed he should just stay home through December and get plenty of rest and relaxation.

Savoring his newfound solitude, Ricky spent hours every day walking around his farm, looking things over, puttering, and fixing things. But at night he still turned to alcohol; he drank his wine and often fell into bed drunk.

The next morning he would say, "I've got to quit drinking. That's it, no more!" But as evening came on, Bettye would watch with a sinking heart as he reached again for his bottle of wine. A week before Christmas Bettye invited Steve and Andy over for a little celebration; her long phone conversations with Andy had dropped off since Ricky's return; besides, she was hoping to do a little fence-mending between Ricky and Steve.

It rained heavily that day, turning the front yard to mud. The black ooze seeped over the little stepping stones that served as a sidewalk from the driveway to the front porch. Ricky looked out at the mud and said, "We can't let them slog up to the house through that stuff." He promptly went out and bought some treated two-by-four lumber and built a sidewalk so Steve and Andy wouldn't get their feet wet that evening.

In spite of a roaring fire and a brightly decorated tree, the atmosphere was more polite than festive. The four exchanged gifts, but conversation was forced and low-key. Relations between Ricky and Steve remained strained, as were relations between Andy and Steve.

"I want so much to see Steve and Ricky rekindle the love and respect they had for each other," Andy told Bettye privately when they went to the kitchen for coffee and carrot cake.

"So do I," said Bettye as she cut slices of the moist, crumbly cake and put them on plates. "I can tell they're both hurting. I know Buck feels that Ricky let him down."

"Steve thinks I let him down too," said Andy, pouring the coffee. "He feels betrayed because I didn't tell him where Ricky was."

"Oh, Andy, I never meant to put you in that position!"

"I know. Don't blame yourself. It's something we have to work out between the two of us. Meanwhile, it looks like things are better with you and Ricky. He seems different somehow. More subdued, but gentle and attentive. This is the first time I've seen the two of you together in your home in over a year."

Bettye put a fork on each plate and reached for the napkins. "Yes, we've been closer since he came home. But he's still drinking heavily. He's hurting and struggling, and there's still a part of him I can't reach, Andy. I don't know what to do. I just pray that God can reach him before it's too late."

Andy clasped Bettye's hand and said firmly, "You remember what we've prayed for all these months. God is faithful, Bettye. He's got Ricky in the palm of His hand, and He's not going to let him go. One of these days He's going to pick him up by his bootstraps and make him into the man He wants him to be. It's going to happen, Bettye. Don't you doubt it for a minute."

"Oh, Andy, what would I do without you? Bettye's eyes glistened with sudden tears. "Andy, we'll need your prayers," she said as she picked up two plates of carrot cake. "Especially when we go home to Virginia for Christmas. Last year was a disaster. Who knows what this year will bring?"

On December 22, Ricky and Bettye drove home to Virginia for the holidays. The next evening they stopped by the home of Ricky's friend, Ronnie, a big, robust man;

246

Ricky and Ronnie had played together in a country band when Ricky lived in Virginia. "Listen, man, we can't stay," Ricky told him at the door. "We just wanted to say hi and drop off a few Christmas presents."

"No way! You can't go yet," said Ronnie as he and his girlfriend, Lynn, beckoned them inside.

Ricky eyed the festive bottles of liquor on the table. "I suppose we can stay long enough for a little Christmas cheer."

"Ricky, we can't," Bettye protested. "It looks like they're getting ready to have their Christmas dinner tonight. It's a family time for them."

"That's okay," said Ronnie. "It's just my parents, sisters, and their husbands, everyone you know. You gotta stay. They'd all love to see you again."

Ricky nodded. "Sure, Ronnie, we'll party a little."

"Great! There's all kinds of food at the buffet table. And plenty of booze. Help yourselves."

Ricky did just that, downing one drink after another. Ronnie's other guests arrived, along with a few people Ricky and Bettye didn't know; they dropped in to say Merry Christmas and decided to stay. Bettye had a feeling they were staying to watch the famous Ricky Van Shelton make a fool of himself. Her anger flared and she wanted to cry out, "Go away! Stop watching my husband like he's some circus sideshow!"

The more intoxicated Ricky became, the more disturbed Bettye grew. She tugged at his arm as he poured another drink, the bottle unsteady in his hands. "Come on, Ricky," she urged with growing frustration. "You said we were just going to stay a minute."

He pulled away, shaking off her hand with an exaggerated gesture. "No, no, no! We're gonna party, Bettye."

"You'll get sick, Ricky. You're drinking on an empty stomach."

"Okay, then I'll eat." He sauntered over to the buffet table, picked up a biscuit, and examined it, holding it close to his eye. "What kind of biscuit is this?"

"Those are angel biscuits," said Ronnie offhandedly. "My mom made them. Try them; they're good."

"Oh, no! No angel biscuits for me!" Ricky pitched the biscuit against the wall as if it were a softball. "Get them angel biscuits away from me!" He ran his hands over several other platters, fumbling among the sandwiches and scattering olives and radishes. "Where are those devils at?" he demanded, his words slurring. At last he seized a deviled egg between his fingers and held it up as if it were a trophy. "Here's what I want. I want *deviled eggs!*"

Everyone laughed, as if he had told a marvelous joke.

Silently Bettye noted, *Ricky is under so much conviction. A battle's raging inside him. The devil is fighting tooth and nail for his soul. It's like this is the final battle over this man!*

Ricky ate his deviled eggs and licked the fluffy yoke from his fingers.

"That's enough, Ricky," Bettye said at last. "You've had your food. Let's go." With a firm hand she steered him away from the table. Everybody was watching, wide-eyed and silent. Ronnie's parents sat around the kitchen table. What must they think? Bettye wondered. They were dignified, mannerly, church-going people. She led Ricky toward the door, urging, "Come on, it's time to go."

"I'm not done partying," he complained, shaking off her grip. Suddenly he lost his balance, stumbled backward, and fell into the lap of Ronnie's laughing mother. He remained on her lap, grinning, as if the whole incident were hilariously funny.

Bettye sighed in resignation. *Ricky's the life of the party . . . but how long will it last?*

Somehow she managed to get Ricky to the door again; but this time he broke away and ran outside and started darting back and forth from one side of the yard to the other. Ronnie's parents and several others went to the door and looked out. "What's he doing out there?" asked Ronnie's mother.

"Looks like he's letting off steam," said Ronnie's father. "Probably been under too much stress, so he's running it out of his system."

"But it's cold out there." Ronnie's mother stepped out on the porch and called, "Ricky, you'd better come back in. You'll catch your death of cold out there!"

Bettye watched in silence. *No use trying to control Ricky; it won't work. He's running from God as fast as he can. And I can't sugar-coat his behavior or save his pride. I'd just get in God's way, and He has a job to do on Ricky.*

After a few minutes Ronnie's parents and guests turned their attention to other things. Their merriment continued until a sudden commotion sounded out in the yard. This time everyone ran outside in alarm.

Bettye—and all of Ronnie's party guests—stared in shock at the bizarre image of her strapping husband climbing up the side of Ronnie's house. "Ricky, come on down!" shouted Ronnie. "This isn't funny, man. You'll kill yourself!"

"Be careful! Don't fall!" several others shouted.

Ignoring the chorus of admonitions, Ricky sprang from the sun deck to the drain pipe, then hoisted himself up onto a railing. He stood balanced on the railing for a long moment, then extended one hand into the air, reaching for the roof. Suddenly he wobbled, lost his footing, and came crashing down to the ground.

Everyone stared in horror at Ricky lying on his back in a dazed stupor amid the revolting, unsavory contents of a ruptured trash can. His arms were outstretched, as if in flight, and he was surrounded by tin cans, bottles, fish heads, chicken bones, newspapers, and assorted items of questionable origin.

Bettye ran to him and helped him to his feet as Ronnie and his guests crowded around, everyone expressing concern at once. "Ricky, why in the world did you want to climb on my house?" cried Ronnie. "You could have killed yourself!"

Ricky brushed the debris from his jeans and stomped back toward the deck. "I gotta get on the roof," he declared, as if he were making perfect sense. "I wanna yell across the valley. I gotta get up there and yell, Ronnie. Just get me on the roof and let me yell."

Ronnie strode over, gripped Ricky by the arm, and led him back into the house. "You gotta stay off my house, man."

Ricky dragged his feet and shook his head. "No, Ronnie, I wanna yell on the roof. I just gotta yell!"

Bettye noticed that no one was laughing at Ricky anymore. All eyes showed sadness and pity. The party broke up shortly after Ricky's near escapade on the roof. People gathered their things and began to leave. Finally everyone had gone home except Ronnie, Lynn, Bettye, and Ricky.

Ricky was as wired as ever, pacing the floor, swinging his arms.

"How do you calm this guy down?" Ronnie asked Bettye. He sounded concerned.

"I don't know," she sighed. "I've never seen him this bad before."

"Look at him," said Ronnie with growing dismay. "He looks unconscious, like he's already passed out, but he won't stop moving. I don't know how he keeps on his feet. I've never seen anything like it."

Bettye shook her head. "I don't think I can get him home like this. What should I do?"

"Let's see if we can get him to the back bedroom. Maybe he'll sleep it off."

Between the two of them they coaxed Ricky into the spare bedroom at the back of the house. Together they managed to get him down on the bed. He lay still for a minute, so Ronnie turned off the light and they began to tiptoe from the room. But as soon as they reached the door, Ricky bounded off the bed and began flailing his arms and screaming. He threw over an amplifier, slammed his fist into the wall, and knocked a stack of boxes onto the floor.

"Stop, Ricky!" cried Bettye. "You're destroying Ronnie's stuff!"

"Man, he's gone berserk," Ronnie exclaimed. "Fightin' and yellin' like a banshee!" He grabbed Ricky by the shoulders, but Ricky threw him off and just kept swinging his arms, sending everything within reach careening from one wall to the other.

Ronnie tackled him again and wrestled him onto the bed. "Stop, man! Ricky, you're gonna hurt yourself!"

Ricky continued to struggle, shaking his head from side to side, heaving his torso, and kicking the footboard with his leather boots, but Ronnie held him firm. "Calm down, man. That's it, Ricky, calm down."

As Ricky settled down, Ronnie looked over at Bettye in the doorway. "What's wrong with him? What is he fighting so hard?" He sounded worried, scared. "We were good drinkin' buddies for years and I never saw nothin' like this!"

She shook her head despairingly. "Oh, Ronnie, I know, I know!"

Ricky struggled to sit up, swayed back and forth for a moment, then collapsed back on the mattress. Ronnie reached for a guitar near the bed and began to strum it. The soft, gentle melody seemed to soothe Ricky's troubled spirit.

Bettye sat down on the floor at the foot of the bed and watched for what seemed hours as that big, gentle man sat in the shadows playing his guitar and singing softly to Ricky. At about three o'clock in the morning Ronnie stood up and put his guitar aside. "He's passed out cold, Bettye. Why don't you get a little shut-eye before morning."

Bettye stood up and gave Ronnie a grateful hug. "Thanks for calming him down. I'm so sorry he—"

"No, don't say it. You just take good care of my buddy, okay? Good night, Bettye."

Quietly she lay down on the narrow bed beside her slumbering husband. There was little room on the mattress, but she pressed her body close to his and gradually

252

matched the rhythm of his breathing. She couldn't sleep —was too keyed up even to relax—but she lay unmoving in the darkness, willing her warmth and closeness to somehow comfort this troubled man she loved so deeply.

At about five in the morning, just as faint rays of sunlight filtered through the venetian blinds, Ricky stirred and mumbled, "It's dark."

"It's okay, Ricky," she whispered back. "It's me. I'm here, baby."

"Where am I?"

"We're at Ronnie's house."

He sat up abruptly. "I've gotta get outta here."

"Okay, we'll go. Just let me tell Ronnie we're leaving."

"No, no! Let's just go."

Without a word they slipped out of the house, drove to the Comfort Inn hotel in Altavista, and checked in. They slept until mid-day, then got up and showered. Ricky was feeling miserable, more hung over than she had ever seen him. He remembered nothing of the night before.

As they dressed, Bettye told him, "Ricky, we need to go and apologize to Ronnie's mother and father."

He looked at her, puzzled. "Why?"

"They were at Ronnie's last night."

"They were?"

"Yeah. We need to call Ronnie, too, and tell him you're all right."

Ricky gave her a blank look. "What did I do, Bettye?"

She shook her head. "I can't begin to tell you how awful it was."

"Don't. Don't tell me. I don't want to know."

SHE STAYS

"No, Ricky. You really do need to know."

"Don't. I was drunk. It's enough."

"No, it's not enough. You need to know what you did last night." In a slow, precise voice she related each incident, describing how Ricky threw food, sat in Ronnie's mother's lap, climbed up the house, and trashed Ronnie's guest room. "There were young people there last night watching the great Ricky Van Shelton, the hugely successful star, falling all over himself," she said quietly. "They stood gaping at you, Ricky, like you were some freak in a sideshow. Is that how you want people to think of you?"

Ricky sat on the edge of the bed, bent over, his elbows on his knees, his head lowered. "Bettye, something's wrong," he agonized. "Something's wrong with me. I don't remember any of that."

She looked him squarely in the eyes. "Ricky, give up alcohol or it will destroy you."

He met her gaze. He had never sounded so solemn. "Pray to God, Bettye, that He'll help me stop drinking." He stood up and put on his black leather motorcycle jacket with the silver stars on the shoulder.

She followed him to the door. "Where are you going, Ricky?"

"Out to the truck. I gotta drive around and think, Bettye. I gotta be alone. I'll be back when I get things figured out."

She wanted to tell him to wait. He shouldn't be driving yet; he was still shaken from his ordeal last night. But she remembered Andy's words, *Leave him in God's hands, Bettye.* "I'll be praying, Ricky," she told him as he strode out the door.

Almost two hours later Ricky returned. There was a bounce in his step and a spark in his eyes. She went to him and ran her palm over the curve of his cheekbone. "What happened, Ricky?"

His green eyes shone with excitement. "I drove around and talked to God, Bettye. I begged Him to take away my desire for alcohol. This time I asked from my heart instead of my mouth. And God answered my prayer! I felt the desire leave my body. It was like God plucked a big black bird off my shoulder. It's gone, Bettye. I'm free!"

A thought stirred in Bettye's memory. *Ricky will be fine by Christmas,* Andy had predicted. Was she right? Had God truly delivered her husband from alcohol? Ricky did seem different this time. Could she really believe this wasn't just one more promise that would soon be broken?

*A*s the first two weeks of January, 1992, rolled by, Andy began to feel a void in her life; she and Bettye were no longer meeting together for prayer; they rarely even talked on the phone anymore. Andy resisted the impulse to telephone, knowing that Bettye was working on her marriage and devoting herself to her husband.

When at last Andy did telephone, Bettye sounded high-spirited and hopeful. "Oh, Andy, I have such good news. Ricky hasn't had a drink in over three weeks! God took away his desire for alcohol. He's been fine since Christmas, just like you said he would be."

"Oh, that's wonderful, Bettye! God is good!"

"He is, Andy. And He's not finished yet. Ricky asked me for a Bible, and he sits reading it all the time. If he's not reading his Bible, he's watching Christian television. He doesn't say much, but I can see God turning him around."

Andy welcomed the news with a grateful heart. Wasn't this what she and Bettye had prayed for for so many months? God had honored their hours of fervent intercession. Ricky was looking to God for help; and the icing on the cake was that he and Bettye were putting their marriage back together.

But if things were finally going so right, why was Andy suddenly feeling so empty, so at loose ends? Her endometriosis was bad every month now, giving her a lot of pain, but what she was feeling now was more than that.

After Andy hung up the phone, she thought, *God is working a miracle for Bettye and Ricky, but not for Steve and me. We're at an impasse. I'm wearing his engagement ring; we're planning our wedding in March; and yet I'm losing him.*

Andy sat down on the bed in her small rented room and thought about happier days when she first came to Nashville and fell in love with Steve. He was a man of great detail and focus, thoughtful and tender, an historian at heart. Since she commuted between Los Angeles and Nashville, their romance spanned an entire continent. He was constantly writing her little notes saying, *I can't wait to show you Nashville the next time you come to town. . . . I want you to see the battlefields where the War Between the States took place. . . . I can't wait to show you Elvis's guitar or this place or that on Music Row. . . . Wait until I tell you what happened when Patsy Cline appeared at this certain club in town.*

Andy was feeling more optimistic the next week when she flew to Los Angeles to meet with one of her writing partners to work on a new song for Warner/Chappell Music. She and Steve would have a little breather, and she would be seeing her family and longtime friends; that always made her feel better.

Her first few days back in her cozy apartment were pleasant and filled with nostalgia. In the early mornings she meandered up and down familiar streets, chatted with neighbors, and strolled to the corner coffee shop for breakfast.

By the fourth morning she felt as if she were truly home again; the temperature was in the seventies and the sun radiated an exhilarating warmth. At the coffee shop Andy met Mayra, a close friend for over twelve years. They had a leisurely breakfast together, sipping coffee, reminiscing about old times, and catching up on the latest news. Andy told her about her approaching wedding and about the exquisite Victorian house she and Steve were building outside of Nashville.

Finally Andy said, "I'm heading back to my apartment. Breakfast was a little heavy, and my stomach is turning a few somersaults."

Andy's nausea worsened as she walked the short distance to her apartment. *It's just my emotions,* she told herself as she unlocked the door and stepped inside. *Or maybe not!* She felt a sudden revulsion shoot from her stomach into her throat. She ran for the bathroom and made it just in time. She couldn't stop vomiting.

Finally, doubled over in pain, she made her way to the phone and called for her friend Heidi. Weak and drenched in sweat, she spent the next hour in the bathroom, shaking violently and in the throes of dry heaves. After what seemed forever she heard Heidi's frantic knock on the door.

Andy dragged herself across the living room and summoned enough strength to open the door. She could see the shock in Heidi's face. "Oh, Andy, you're white as a ghost!" Before Andy could utter a sound, Heidi took charge; she phoned her doctor, then put her arm around

Andy and helped her outside to her automobile. When they arrived at the hospital shortly after noon, Heidi helped Andy out of the car, into the lobby, and down the hall to the elevator, barking at anyone who got in their way. Every few feet Andy stopped and leaned against the wall, gasping for breath.

The next hour was an agonizing blur for Andy as Heidi's gynecologist examined her and asked countless questions. Finally, as he scribbled something on the chart, he announced that she had suffered a ruptured cyst on an ovary. "You'll need surgery as soon as possible," the physician continued with little change of expression.

"How long will it take to recover?" Andy asked weakly. "I'm getting married in two months."

"Oh, no, you're not," the doctor shot back. "Unless you're prepared to feel miserable at your wedding, I strongly suggest you postpone the date."

Andy felt her emotions unraveling like a ball of string. She had had enough! She put her head in her hands and sobbed. Between stabs of pain she choked out, "You don't understand! No one understands!"

The physician was writing again on her chart. Without looking up he said, "You've been treated previously for severe endometriosis, haven't you, Miss Landis?"

She sniffed noisily and nodded, still wincing with cramps. "Several gynecologists have recommended—they said I needed a hysterectomy. But I couldn't—not yet—!"

"There is a hormone treatment you might consider. It would keep you from ovulating; however, it would take months and give you hot flashes and possibly depression."

259

I don't need drugs to make me depressed, Andy thought darkly.

"Basically you would be experiencing a drug-induced menopause." He paused meaningfully. "I assume you've been told your chances of having children are slim to none."

"Yes, but I—I guess I haven't really believed it—until now." She doubled over again in a knifelike spasm. "Please, doctor, I can't take this pain anymore! Do anything to make the pain stop!"

He nodded. "I'll give you something for the pain and we'll schedule the surgery for later this week."

———◆———

Steve arrived from Nashville the day before Andy's surgery, in time to accompany her to her appointment with the gynecologist. Andy was still feeling weak, exhausted, and defeated; she couldn't eat and was still fighting nausea.

The doctor called them both into his office, invited them to sit down, and told them what to expect. Finally he cautioned, "You understand, Mr. Buckingham, we may have to perform a hysterectomy, depending on how serious the scarring is."

Steve nodded and reached for Andy's hand.

"Even if the hysterectomy is unnecessary, it's unlikely your fiancee will ever be able to have a child."

Andy began to weep.

"She's told me before," said Steve, "but I must admit that until now I didn't fully realize how she feels about it."

The physician folded his hands on his desk. "For now,

260

let's concentrate on the surgery at hand. Do you have any questions?"

In the next half hour Steve proceeded to ask a number of pertinent questions that hadn't occurred to Andy— about the operation itself, the type of anesthesia, possible complications, estimated recovery time, and other details aimed at guaranteeing Andy optimum care. *Amazing!* she thought. *He knows just the right questions to ask!*

An insight struck her. All of Steve's traits that drove her crazy sometimes—his bluntness, his intellect, his memory, his ingenuity, his drive—were the very traits she treasured at this moment.

She noticed that whenever the doctor spoke, he addressed his remarks to Steve, and Steve was taking charge as if it were the most natural thing in the world. He was watching out for her, protecting and taking care of her, and it felt wonderful. He kept her hand firmly in his, as if imparting his strength to her. Suddenly she understood. He was her lifeline; she didn't have to face a precarious future alone. He was in her life to stay!

As they left the medical facility, Steve remained solicitous, supporting her with his arm, helping her into his rental car. Before he started the engine he looked over at her and said, "We really do need each other, Andy. It makes me feel good to know I can be here for you. I didn't realize how good it would feel to have you depending on me."

Andy was silent all the way home, mulling over what Steve had just said. She knew from helping Bettye how good it felt to be strong for somebody else. Had she denied Steve the chance to be strong for her? She wouldn't make that mistake now; she had never needed Steve more.

The next morning he was with her before surgery and sitting at her bedside when she came out of recovery. "You're going to be fine, honey," he told her. "They did the laparoscopy, not the hysterectomy."

When she was discharged two days later, Steve picked her up at the hospital. "We're not going back to your apartment," he announced. "I'm checking you into a hotel."

"But why? My apartment may be small, but I can get by."

"No," he insisted. "You need plenty of bed rest. You're going to have a nice place to recuperate, where you can just buzz room service when you're hungry." He cast her a sidelong glance. "Besides, you know my culinary skills leave a lot to be desired."

When the time approached for Steve to return to Nashville, he and Andy agreed she should finish recuperating at her mother's in Escondido. The day before his flight he packed her things in the trunk of his rental car and they headed south on Interstate 5 along the scenic California coastline. Andy wore an oversized hunter-green sweater over a pair of black leggings, and her flaxen hair was pinned up loosely with Chinese chopsticks decorated with white mother-of-pearl. No more nightshirts or ugly hospital gowns; she was trying to get back to the land of the living. She wasn't there yet, but she could see it in the distance!

As Steve drove, he reached over and took her hand. Keeping his gaze on the road, he said, "I know you're disappointed about postponing our wedding, Andy."

"Yes, I am," she answered softly. "I can't help feeling like nothing ever goes right for us."

"I know, honey. We've faced some hard times in our relationship. Look at us; we're so different. I'm organized, stubborn, set in my ways, maybe too predictable. You, Andy—you're an adventurer—unusual, spontaneous, unpredictable. I'm methodical, a planner; you get brainstorms that send you off in every direction at once."

She looked over at him. "What are you trying to tell me, Steve?"

He met her gaze and smiled. "Just that it takes some getting used to having you in my life, because I never know what's going to happen next. But please be patient with me, Andy. I really believe you are the right person for me. I need you, honey, and I want you to be my wife. As soon as the doctor gives you the okay, we'll set a new date. You plan the wedding the way you envision it, and I'll do everything I can to help."

Andy gratefully pressed his hand against her cheek. Tears welled in her eyes. She felt safe now; it was okay to need this special man God had brought into her life. "Thank you, Steve," she murmured, her voice catching with emotion. "I love you more than I can say."

Still holding his hand, she turned her gaze out the window to the sun-spangled ocean that stretched to a clear, cloud-free horizon and wondered, *Is it really possible my future with Steve could be like that—clear and cloud-free?*

CHAPTER 27

While Andy was facing surgery in Los Angeles, Bettye and Ricky spent the last half of January quietly on their farm. Every day Bettye saw new ways that God was dealing with Ricky. He had asked for a Bible and she had given him one; now he was examining other versions as well so that he could read and compare the meanings of various passages. Sometimes he talked with her about what he had read or asked what she thought something meant. But mostly he just sat and read quietly, hour after hour.

When he wasn't reading the Scriptures, he was sitting in his recliner watching Christian television. At first he flipped from one station to another, from CBN to TBN to another Christian channel and back again, watching a few minutes of one program and then another. As the days passed, he began watching entire programs; and before long he was tuning regularly to several evangelists and listening intently to their messages.

Bettye said little during these days, knowing that what was happening had to be between God and Ricky. Sometimes she opened her mouth to offer an opinion or give

Ricky a spiritual nudge, but God would shut her mouth. *I guess that's how we women are,* she mused to herself. *We want to take control and fix and mend and nurture. But it'll take a whole lot longer if I try to get in the middle of it.*

One day late in January, Ricky, in his usual T-shirt and jeans, came striding into the living room and approached Bettye with a curious expression—a look of tenderness, remorse, hope, and excitement. She was sitting near the window in the royal blue, overstuffed mohair chair with the colorful Indian blanket thrown over the back. She was wearing a plain brown cotton dress with a scoop neck, and her auburn hair hung in long ringlets around her face and shoulders.

Ricky gazed down at her and said with a note of wonderment, "Bettye, I want you to know; I just prayed and asked Christ to forgive me of my sins and come back into my life as my Lord and Savior, and He did! It was like God was telling me, 'Okay, okay, I've been here all along!' The burden's gone, Bettye. It's like a thousand-pound boulder was lifted off my shoulders."

For an instant Bettye stared back in astonishment; then she bounded out of her chair and into Ricky's arms. They held each other for a long while. She had prayed fervently for this moment for over a year, and the Lord had answered her prayer. "Thank God, Ricky," she said aloud. "Praise Jesus!"

"God is so faithful, Bettye. I left Him, but He never left me. If He had, I would have been dead by now." He smiled and tapped his forehead. "You know what, Bettye? Every day God is filling my mind with His Word. This ol' head used to be a beer mug, but now it's a cup, and the Spirit's filling it up with the Word of God!"

She laughed lightly, still in the circle of his arms. "That's right! We don't need any beer mugs around this house anymore."

"No, we don't," he said expansively. "I ain't had a beer since before Christmas, and I don't want a beer now. I trust God I'll never want a beer again!"

He glanced around the room as if he were looking for something. "Bettye, do we have some writing paper around here?"

She looked blankly at him. "Sure, Ricky. Why do you want writing paper?"

He ran his hand back through his light-brown, shoulder-length hair. "I want to write some of those TV preachers and thank them for pointing me back to Jesus. They helped turn my life around, so I want to tell them so. I gotta be real honest with them, Bettye, and tell about the alcoholism and the infidelities, so they'll know what they helped save me from."

"I understand, Ricky. I'll get you some stationery and you write whatever you feel God is telling you to write."

"Thanks, Bettye." A glint of sadness flickered in his eyes. He ran his hands lightly over her bare arms and his tone turned somber. "I've been thinking, Bettye. I feel really bad now about the women I got drunk with and slept with. I sure wish I could apologize to them."

Bettye flinched and drew away from her husband's embrace. She sat back down in the mohair chair. "You want to apologize to those women you were with?" she asked carefully, a wrenching ache suddenly marring her joy.

Ricky's brow furrowed. "Yeah, I really regret what I

SHELTON & LANDIS

did. I only did it when I was sloppy, stupid drunk. But I'm so sorry. I wish I could tell them so."

She looked up at him, pressure building behind her eyes. "Ricky, you never apologized to *me!*"

He stared down at her in disbelief, his eyes narrowing. "You mean I never told you I was sorry for what happened?" He sat down on the wide arm of her chair close to her and ran his hand over her shoulder and through her crimped curls. He was silent for several minutes. Finally he spoke, his voice breaking with emotion. "Bettye, I don't know how you could ever forgive me for what I've put you through this past year." He shook his head mournfully. "How can it ever be right between us after all I've done to hurt you?"

She smiled faintly. Those were the sweetest words she had ever heard. She looked up at him and said, "Ricky, we don't need to go back to what we had. It's going to be better between us than it ever was. I thank God it won't be the same. Don't you see? I can forgive everything. Is that what you want?"

He sat down cross-legged on the floor by her chair. His ruddy forehead glistened and the muscles along his jaw tightened with a vivid intensity. "It is, Bettye. I want to make it right between us again as husband and wife. Do you forgive me?"

She reached down and touched his face with her fingertips. "I do, Ricky. I love you."

He caught her hand and locked fingers with hers. "And I love you, wife." He grinned. "That's biblical, you know."

"What is?"

"Biblical men called their wives, 'wife.' Like Abraham and Sarah."

"I like it," said Bettye. "It makes me feel like we really belong to each other, the way God intended."

Ricky stood up and held out his arms. His green eyes crinkled merrily. "Wife, come here!"

"Yes, husband." She stood up and went eagerly into his arms, savoring his warmth and closeness.

"I love you, wife," he whispered against her cheek. He tilted her chin up to his and kissed her lips gently, tenderly, the way she had yearned for so long to be kissed by her husband.

———◦◦◦———

After two agonizing months of hormone shots, night sweats, and hot flashes, Andy was beginning to feel better by March. Her body was healing; her spirits were lifting; her faith was stronger, for God had walked with her through her valley of shadows. Her relationship with Steve was closer than it had ever been, and her career was in high gear as she began recording songs for her own album with Star Song.

Andy had even come to see a symbolic meaning in her surgery. Not just physical scars, but emotional scars had been burned away, leaving her feeling cleansed and healthy in mind as well as body. Well enough, in fact, to prepare for her wedding. Yes, the date was set—again! On May 2, 1992, she would marry Steve Buckingham in beautiful La Jolla, California.

During March and April Andy expended every ounce of energy shopping for her dress, sending out invitations, making flight reservations, and planning her ceremony.

She lined up several musician friends from Nashville to play classical music, invited Bettye to participate in the candlelighting ceremony, and planned her own flower arrangements and bouquets. Everything was coming together just the way she hoped. Her father would walk her down the aisle; her sisters Diana and Jennifer would serve as her bridesmaids; and her sister Anita would tend to the four nephews and nieces who would take part in the ceremony.

In mid-April Andy flew to California to take care of last-minute details. For the next two weeks she commuted between her Los Angeles apartment and her mother's home in Escondido. On April 22 her wedding preparations were interrupted by a 6.1 magnitude earthquake in southern California, followed three days later by the big 6.9 quake that shook Northern California and jarred frayed nerves in the L.A. basin as well.

Besides enduring several days of aftershocks, Andy found herself driving from L.A. to Escondido the very day the Los Angeles riots broke out. Steve arrived in southern California the next day, April 30, while the nation stared in horror at TV screens showing violence, anarchy, and flames devastating scores of Los Angeles communities. Andy kept one eye glued to the TV as she prepared for her wedding. With every hour the violence escalated. She realized how close to home the riots had come when she recognized a familiar landmark on her television screen. The theater a block and a half from her house was on fire; the violence had reached her own neighborhood!

Although the riots kept scores of people from attending Andy's wedding, the atmosphere in the La Jolla Presbyterian Church on that May 2nd afternoon was marked by tranquillity, joy, and deep sentiment as nearly one hundred of Steve and Andy's family and friends gathered to celebrate their marriage.

The ceremony began at four in the afternoon with Bettye and Andy's former roommate Liz walking down the aisle in matched cadence and lighting the candelabra. Privately, from the vestibule Andy watched Bettye and reflected on all they had been through together. *What a blessing she is!* Andy marveled. *I'm so glad I stretched myself to be her friend.*

As the organ struck up the wedding march, Andy moved down the long aisle on her father's arm. She wore a gown of embroidered satin, pearls, and lace, with a form-fitting bodice and sleeves puffed at the shoulders and tapered at the wrist. Her veil framed her face in a cloud of white netting and her flaxen hair cascaded over her shoulders and hung in ringlets along her cheekbones. Her green eyes danced with excitement.

Steve was waiting for her at the altar, tall and imposing in his black tuxedo, black cummerbund, white shirt, and black bow tie. His dark hair was naturally styled and his classically sculpted features possessed a solemn but robust vitality.

Andy took her place beside her fiancé and they faced the minister, a tall, dark, bearded man with a receding hairline. In a deep, resonant voice he declared, "Dear friends, we are gathered here this afternoon to share with Cynthia Landis and Steven Buckingham a very important moment in their lives. It seems good and right that they should be joined together as husband and wife, for their love has been proved, and now they wish to make a public commitment of that love to their family and friends."

Steve stood unmoving, watching the minister as he spoke, but Andy watched Steve. She had eyes for no one else.

After the wedding, Andy had the reception of her dreams at the resplendent La Valencia Hotel. The reception room overlooked bountiful gardens of lush flowers, and beyond them the deep blue Pacific stretched to the horizon.

In the midst of the celebration, Bettye approached and offered a loving embrace and her own congratulations. "Buck and Andy—*Mrs.* Buckingham—I'm so glad I was here, and that I came a day early and got to spend time with your family. I got to know them and share their feelings, so when I looked around the church tonight, I knew your mother and father, and your sisters and your brothers-in-law; I knew them in my spirit, and that's so special to me. Thank you so much.

"I just want you to know I called Ricky on the road before I came to the wedding, and he's here in spirit with us too. He said to tell you, 'God bless you both.' He's praying for a wonderful life for the two of you."

Bettye turned to go, then paused and squeezed Andy's hand. Andy noted that Bettye had never looked more beautiful, nor possessed greater poise and confidence. With a beaming smile, Bettye added in a confidential voice, "And thank you, Andy, for standing with me, no matter what. No matter what."

*I*n June, 1992, Bettye and Ricky had a decision to make. Actually, it was Ricky's decision; Bettye was careful about that. Over the months Ricky had struck up a telephone friendship with one of the TV evangelists he had written, and now the evangelist was inviting the two of them to attend an upcoming conference. The idea was tempting. They could come anonymously, sit in the audience, and just enjoy the service and soak up the teaching. It would be very low key; no one would announce that they were there.

Ricky said he would need a few days to think and pray about it. It would be a big step in his new walk of faith—and a giant step as well in his marriage. As youngsters, he and Bettye had been in church every time the doors were opened, but they hadn't attended a church service together in their entire married life!

Several days passed before Ricky approached Bettye in the kitchen one afternoon, and said, "Make the arrangements. Get us some plane tickets. We're going to the conference."

She brightened immediately. "We are?"

"Yeah. I feel like the Lord is telling me to go."

"All right!" Bettye had been hoping and praying for this answer, but hadn't wanted to push. She savored the way Ricky was becoming the spiritual head of their home, and she didn't want to do anything that would undermine his position of leadership.

For months she had marveled over the way God was working in their lives. Since Ricky's commitment to Christ in January, he had faithfully studied his Bible, whether at home, in his bus, or in a hotel room in some far-flung state. Often he called and reminded Bettye of key Scripture verses just when she needed reminding, or he asked her to pray with him about matters he felt needed prayer. Many times they got down on their knees beside their four-poster bed and held hands while each of them prayed. Sometimes he read the Bible to her in bed, and if she dozed off, he would shake her and wake her up. "Bettye, this is important," he'd declare. "Wake up! You've got to hear this!"

And she'd say, "Yes, husband, yes, husband. I'm awake."

They spent precious times talking about what was in the Bible and trying to better understand some of its mysteries. There was so much to discuss, so much to learn about what God had to tell them in His Word. Ricky was the seeker now. "I'm just gonna stay in God's face all the time," he said, "until I know what He wants me to know."

And now, to Bettye's delight, Ricky was willing to attend a Christian conference that would bring people of faith together from all over the world. Neither of them had any idea what to expect, but on Wednesday, June 17,

1992, they boarded their flight out of Nashville; they both sensed that God had extraordinary blessings in store for them.

After settling into an elegant guest house stocked with food and reserved just for them, Bettye and Ricky made their way to the evening worship service. The program was full, with lots of soul-stirring music and several prominent ministers scheduled to speak. As promised, Bettye and Ricky were allowed to sit in the audience and blend in with the crowd—a rare treat for Ricky.

That is, until the final guest evangelist finished his message. While dozens of people streamed to the altar for prayer, the evangelist unknowingly singled out Bettye and Ricky, and commanded, "Come here, brother. You and your wife, come here!"

They immediately stood as one and made their way to the platform. It never occurred to them to do anything but go forward. As they approached the evangelist, he told the crowd, "I don't know who this man is, but God has a mighty calling on his life."

He turned to Ricky and said, "God's got something for you, brother. The Lord tells me you've been in the entertainment field."

A titter of recognition rippled across the audience. The evangelist smiled and said, "You're still in entertainment? Well, God is about to put you on a launching pad. You think you've seen things, but you've seen nothing yet. The Lord is changing your entire career."

He stretched his hand toward Ricky. "Give me your hand, you and your wife both." They drew close, bowing their heads and closing their eyes as he clasped their hands. "I feel so strongly that God is changing your career, putting you literally on a launching pad like the space shuttle. He's going to take you to a brand new location and you'll bless a lot of people. You'll lose nothing, but you'll gain much. God is going to add and add and add. God doesn't take anything away; He just adds.

"Notice, the next few days things will begin to happen in your home and in your heart and in your wife's heart; tremendous things are going to happen."

At mention of their home and hearts, Bettye's lower lip trembled and her chin quivered; she began to weep quietly. She felt Ricky's arm circle her waist and draw her against him. She bent her head close to his shoulder and put her forehead against his cheek for a long moment, weeping.

"You're going to discover the personality of the Spirit in such a way, tremendous things are going to happen with you," the evangelist continued in an exultant voice. "I also see the Lord doing something—I don't understand this, but I'll tell you what I see."

Bettye and Ricky opened their eyes now and fixed their gaze on him. "Brother, I see you wearing what looks like a black robe. The Lord is removing it and replacing it with a white one. Your wife—I see what looks like a gray robe. You haven't been as deep in the darkness as your husband. I see God removing your gray robe and putting on you a white robe. And the people you will talk to, the Lord, through you, will change their robes from black to white, from black to white."

Bettye looked at Ricky, her eyes wet with tears. She couldn't contain the joy she felt. In her mind's eye she was reliving all they had been through the past year and a half. Now they were standing at the altar hand in hand while a man of God pronounced a blessing on them. For the first time in her marriage she felt that she and Ricky were standing as husband and wife before God. A spiritual marriage was taking place between them; this extraordinary moment had been carved out of time and given eternal significance.

To her astonishment she could feel the year and a half of heartache, alienation, and betrayal being washed away. All those months hadn't happened to her and Ricky because the two of them were new people now, dressed in the white robes of Christ's forgiveness. There was nothing else for her to forgive.

Standing at that altar in Ricky's arms, she sensed a powerful truth—she would never look back on what had happened with hurt or bitterness or anger, because it was truly as if it had never happened at all.

Late that night, when Bettye and Ricky returned to their guest house, she felt as if they were still riding the sweet euphoria of the Spirit. Their hearts were buoyant, their energies charged. It was better than young love, because God was at the center of their heightened emotion.

In the comfortable privacy of their luxurious room they dressed for bed and climbed between the covers. Ricky opened his Bible and began to read to her while she cuddled close to him in the crook of his arm. He read for a while, then put the Bible on the nightstand and turned out the bedside lamp. They lay in each other's arms, talking quietly in the darkness, reliving the evening's remarkable events.

"Ricky," she said softly, "I feel like we just got married tonight. I feel like this is our honeymoon."

"I feel the same way," he whispered against her

276

cheek. "You gave me a hundred percent love. You stood by me when I was running around, when I was drunk, when I gave up on myself. You stood by me and loved me and turned me over to God and prayed for me."

He kissed her with exquisite tenderness, gentleness, and desire. "Bettye, I love you more than I can say."

She responded with sweet, rising passion. Running her hand over his smooth temple and through his hair, she said breathlessly, "I love you too, Ricky. This is the way God meant for a husband and wife to feel toward each other."

They made love as if it were the very first time. It was all the wonderful things Bettye had yearned for from her husband and hadn't received. Romance, appreciation, sharing, a physical union ignited by the Spirit and blessed by God.

So this is what marriage is about, Bettye marveled. *This is the way God planned it all along!*

*I*n the spring of 1993, Andy heard a melody in her mind. It began with just a few notes and the words, "She stays." Andy began to hum it over and over. She couldn't get the tune out of her head.

As the measures and lyrics came to her, she knew this would be a song about commitment, about a woman who stayed in a difficult marriage, not out of weakness, but because she believed in the vows she had made to God and her partner.

It was Bettye's story.

Andy was convinced this song belonged on the album she was recording with Star Song. After presenting the idea to her record company, she contacted Allen Shamblin, a successful songwriter, and he helped her finish the song.

The first time Andy performed "She Stays" in concert, she was surprised by the number of women who came up afterward and told her, with tears in their eyes, "You wrote that song for me. It describes my marriage. You've put into words what I sensed in my heart was right —that God wants me to stay and be loving and allow

Him to work in my partner. Thank you for confirming that truth in your song. It gives me hope."

In the months that followed, as Andy traveled all over the United States and Europe performing, "She Stays," she noticed a phenomenal thing happening. At every concert, women of every age and description grew teary-eyed or began to weep, and after the show they came up and thanked her for that song. Over and over again they told her, "You've captured just how I feel. You've made me feel less alone. You've confirmed the rightness of my decision to stay." And the letters began to pour in from women—and men!—everywhere who had felt, at times, like the woman in the song.

It became apparent that this story was bigger than just Bettye's or Andy's experience. Bettye's struggle was being replayed over and over again in the lives of people everywhere who had to decide whether to leave a troubled marriage or, by God's grace, to stay. As Bettye and Andy shared with others the story of their friendship and the restoration of Bettye's marriage, they caught a glimpse of the good that could be accomplished by women helping women to stay in their marriages and to stand firm in their faith.

Ultimately, this is a story of commitment—a commodity desperately needed but rarely applauded today. Bettye and Andy want to help change that. That's why they've told their story, and that's why "She Stays" is Andy's favorite song to sing. She dedicates this song to all the men and women whose faith, courage, and commitment may never be known to anyone but God, but who know that there are times when God calls them to stay.

279

She Stays

Andy Landis and Allen Shamblin

She'd give anything to hear him say he loves her
Seems like years since he told her so
And she longs for the way he used to hold her
Just when the fire burned out . . .
     she doesn't know

In this day and age
She could walk away
No one would blame her

But she stays
She gets down on her knees and she prays
Looks at the ring that he gave her
So one more time
She makes up her mind and
     she stays

She says something deep inside of her is dying
Loneliness cuts her to the bone
But he can't understand the tears she's crying
And that leaves her feeling even more alone

She is strong enough
She could take her love
Go on without him

But she stays
She gets down on her knees and she prays

SHELTON & LANDIS

Looks at the ring that he gave her
So one more time
She makes up her mind and
    she stays

Letting go of a man without leaving his side is so ˈ
    hard, it's so hard
But she believes in her promise
And she's holding on tight with
    her heart, her heart

So she stays
She gets down on her knees and she prays
Looks at the ring that he gave her
So one more time
She makes up her mind and
    she stays
And looks at the ring that he gave her
She knows love will do
What she's asking it to
So she stays

*I*n 1992, Ricky asked me to start up and run his own publishing company, RVS Books, Inc., to release a series of six children's books called *Tales from a Duck Named Quacker*. This has been a major undertaking, with over 150,000 books sold to date.

In December 1992, I finally graduated with honors from Belmont University—a major goal that I have worked toward for almost twenty years!

Together Ricky and I have worked toward creating a parklike environment surrounding our farm. We spend hours of our time cultivating flowers, trees, and shrubs next to the river and around our home. It seems overwhelming at times, but the beauty and harmony of our many flower beds seem well worth our time and energy.

We are also spending more time in Virginia with our families. We now realize how important close family ties are to us and hope to eventually move back to our home area.

When I am not working on the publishing company, gardening, answering fan mail, or traveling with Ricky, I still have our herd of beefalo cattle to manage, along with normal housekeeping duties, such as cleaning, ironing, and cooking.

Andy and I have not spent much time together since 1992; but yet, there is always the knowledge that she is there for me. I can never repay her for answering God's call to help me. She was my lifeline to God.

In December, 1990, I prayed to God to give me back my husband the way he used to be. Since May, 1992, I have learned that God had a better plan for our marriage. I now know the meaning of "marriage in the sight of God." When God is the center for both husband and wife, the love and intimacy between the two are beyond any we ever experienced before.

Ricky and I have shared our testimony with many during the last few years. Through our openness, we have learned that hundreds, even thousands, of men and women are suffering because of broken relationships. They are desperate for hope. With Andy's help, I have learned that God's promises work when we trust Him and live for Him. This is the message I want to share.

A   WORD   FROM
ANDY   LANDIS

*S*o much has happened that it seems a lifetime has passed since May of '92, yet it has flown by.

Steve and I moved into our country home in August 1992. We have filled it with special things, simple treasures, and music. We've planted trees and beautiful flowers. It's been wonderfully healing for both of us. Sometimes when I'm driving up the long gravel road to the farm, I see a glimpse of my home on the hill and feel awestruck that Steve and I actually live there! I'm so grateful.

My health has improved since the surgery. No, we still don't have children. I've had to give all those desires to God. I trust that He has a plan that I am only beginning to understand. But I am living without pain! And, oh, what a difference that has made. I feel . . . normal. (I use the word loosely, of course, because my husband may beg to differ.)

We've lost both Danny (to old age) and Tommy (his leukemia finally did come back) in the last few years. We still think of them and feel blessed to have had them in our lives for a while. Now we have three vivacious dogs to

285

SHE STAYS

keep us company. They were all strays at one time so we do our best to spoil them rotten.

I miss my family; Mom, Dad, my sisters, nieces, and nephews because I live so far away. The distance hasn't lessened our love for one another, however. Our visits just become all the more important and precious.

I don't see Bettye as often as I would like. Still, God has bound us together with a spiritual thread that is unbreakable. I know I can count on her friendship and she knows she can count on mine.

And if I was called to her again, I would do it . . . no matter what.